Student Workbook

Today's Math

Daily Practice

Mixed Review

Test Prep

Editorial Offices: Glenview, Illinois • Parsippany, New Jersey • New York, New York
Sales Offices: Needham, Massachusetts • Duluth, Georgia • Glenview, Illinois
Coppell, Texas • Ontario, California • Mesa, Arizona

Created by Pearson Scott Foresman to supplement **Investigations in Number, Data, and Space®**
These materials do not necessarily reflect the opinions or perspective of TERC or the authors of the
Investigations curriculum.

ISBN: 0-328-12652-7

6 7 8 9 10 V004 13 12 11 10 09 08 07 06 05

Contents

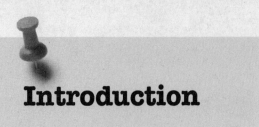

Introduction

Why This Book?

School policies vary widely on issues of homework. Some teachers are free to assign homework as they see fit, while others are required to assign work every night, every other night, or according to some other schedule depending on the age of their students.

In order to accommodate the wide range of school and district policies, enough homework is embedded in the *Investigations* curriculum that a teacher can assign homework about every other night. Furthermore, Practice Pages, Extensions, Classroom Routines (in grades K–2), Ten-Minute Math activities (in grades 3–5), and *Investigations* Games can be used to provide or create additional homework assignments.

Recently, teachers have expressed a need for an additional resource: grade-specific books that will meet three needs:

- Relate to the math content of each day's session

- Provide daily practice in number sense and operations

- Help prepare students for standardized testing

This book meets these needs.

- It provides engaging and meaningful practice that will further develop children's understanding of the basic concepts and skills that are currently being taught.

- It gives parents and other caregivers a better sense of what children are doing in math class and over the course of the school year. Most parents understand that "the basics" now encompass all areas of mathematics, not only arithmetic. And many parents are willing, and indeed eager, to help however they can. Therefore, on all student pages there are **Family Connection** notes that give parents the information they need.

- The **Mixed Review and Test Prep** sections help develop computational fluency while preparing students for the language and format of standardized tests. (These sections review concepts and skills that were taught in the previous grade.)

Family Connection

Dear Family,

Pearson Scott Foresman is pleased to introduce a new component in your child's mathematics program: Today's Math workbooks.

Sometimes your child will complete a page in class and bring it home to show you. Other times, your child might be assigned a page to complete at home (perhaps with your assistance, as time allows).

Features of Today's Math

1 The **main activity** relates to the math content of that day's math lesson (or, in some cases, to previous lessons within the current unit).

2 **Mixed Review and Test Prep** exercises prepare your child for standardized testing. Each test-prep item **(a)** helps your child review and maintain basic number skills and concepts learned previously; and **(b)** helps prepare him or her to deal with, and indeed feel comfortable with, the language and format of standardized tests.

3 The **Family Connection** notes will give you **(a)** a "snapshot" of what your child is doing in math class; **(b)** the background you need in order to help your child; **(c)** opportunities to engage in "math conversations" with your child; and **(d)** suggestions for activities you might do together with your child.

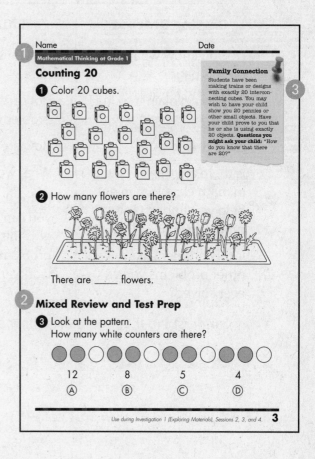

When Working with Your Child

Try using some of the sample questions from the chart below. They can help you start an ongoing math conversation with your child, and they will encourage your child to explain his or her mathematical thinking. It is vitally important that children learn to verbalize their thinking, voice their questions and concerns, and learn to think of themselves as effective and thoughtful problem solvers. Knowing that their parents and teachers value their thinking is very important to children.

We hope that you will enjoy working on Today's Math with your child. As always, your participation and support are greatly valued and very much appreciated.

Having Math Conversations with Your Child

SAMPLE QUESTIONS

Getting Started	While Working	Wrapping Up
• Do you know what to do on this page?	• Do you see any patterns here?	• Why did you decide to solve the problem this way?
• Can you explain it to me?	• How are these two problems alike?	• Is there another way to solve this kind of problem?
• Is there something you need to find out?	• How are they different?	• How do you know that your answer makes sense?
• Is there anything you did in math class that might help you understand this problem?	• What would happen if …?	• What kinds of math problems are easy for you?
• Is this problem like any other problems you've ever solved?	• Is this the kind of problem you can do in your head, or is this the kind of problem you need to work out on paper?	• What kinds of problems are hard for you?

Mathematical Thinking at Grade 1

Where Does It Go?

In which bin would you put
each shape? Write the letter
of the bin under the shape.

Family Connection
Students have been
exploring some of the tools
and materials they will use
as they learn about mathematics this year. They are
working with (a) **interlocking cubes,** which are multi-
colored plastic cubes that
snap together; (b) **pattern
blocks,** which consist of six
two-dimensional shapes,
including yellow hexagons,
red trapezoids, green triangles, orange squares, and
blue and tan rhombuses;
and (c) **Geoblocks,** three-
dimensional shapes that
include rectangular prisms,
square prisms, cubes, trian-
gular prisms, and pyramids.

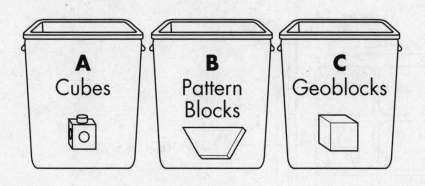

A Cubes   **B** Pattern Blocks   **C** Geoblocks

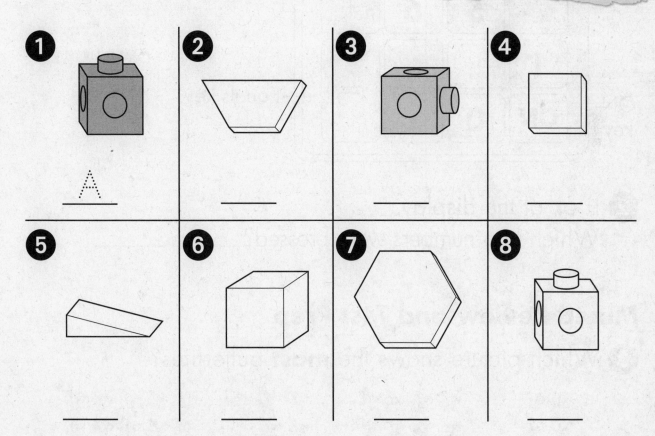

1 A ____

2 ____

3 ____

4 ____

5 ____

6 ____

7 ____

8 ____

Name _____ Date _____

Exploring Calculators

1 Write the missing numbers on the calculator's number keys.

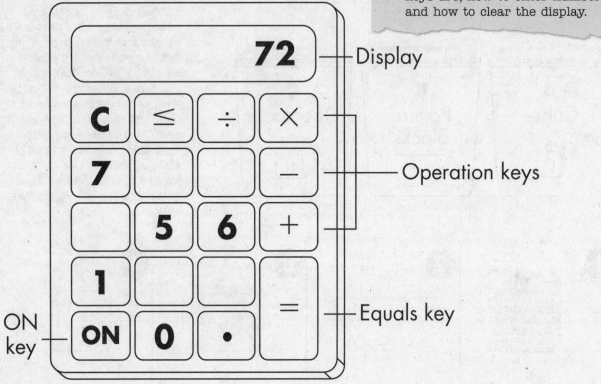

Display

Operation keys

Equals key

ON key

2 Look at the display.
Which two numbers were pressed? _____

Mixed Review and Test Prep

3 Which picture shows the **most** butterflies?

Ⓐ   Ⓑ   Ⓒ   Ⓓ

Name _____   Date _____

Counting 20

1 Color 20 cubes.

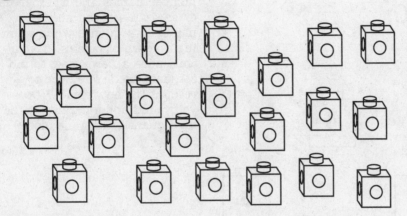

2 How many flowers are there?

There are _____ flowers.

Mixed Review and Test Prep

3 Look at the pattern.
How many white counters are there?

12   8   5   4
Ⓐ   Ⓑ   Ⓒ   Ⓓ

What Is It?

Connect the cubes.
Count from 1 to 20.

Family Connection

Students have been counting groups of objects. Listen to see whether your child knows the number names and whether he or she can say the number names in sequence while counting a group of objects. If your child adds a new object to the set, does he or she need to recount the set from 1? Does your child understand that the total quantity has one more?

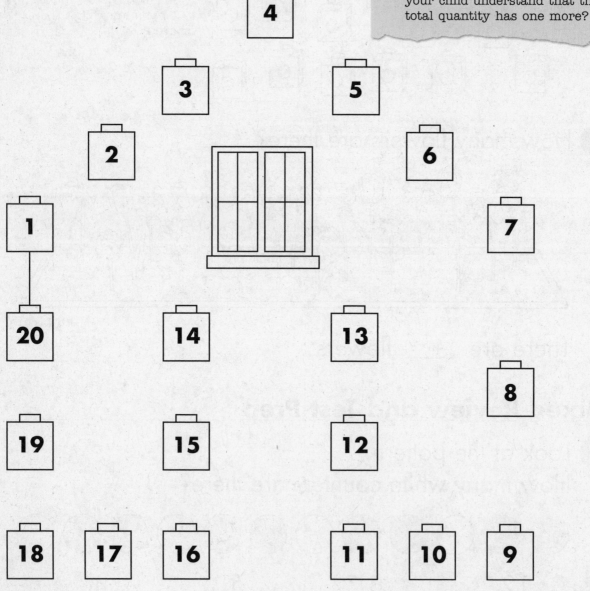

I made a _____ with _____ cubes.

Mathematical Thinking at Grade 1

Which Number Is Larger?

Circle the clown who is balancing more balls.

1

2

3

4

5

6

Make a Staircase

Color squares to make
a staircase.

Then turn this page upside down.
What do you see?

Family Connection

Students have been building
"staircases" using interlocking
cubes and matching them with the
number cards that tell how many
cubes. After your child has
completed coloring the staircase,
ask him or her to tell you the
smallest number and the largest
number and to count from 1 to 12
in order.

_____

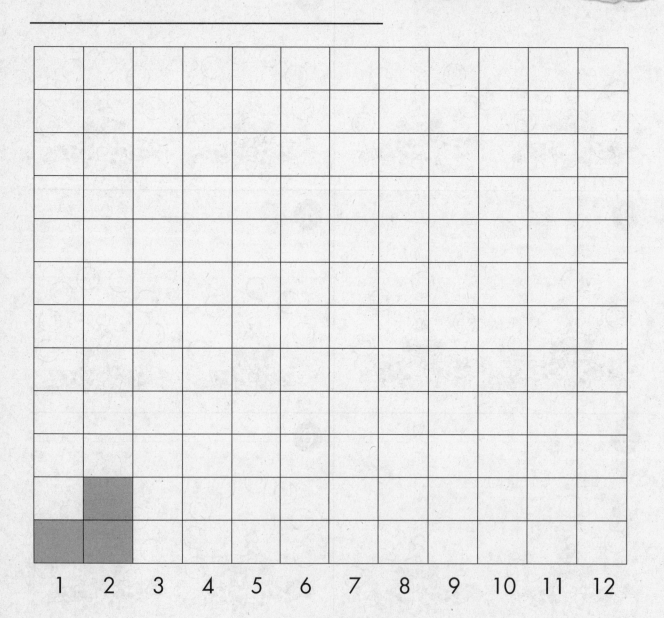

1   2   3   4   5   6   7   8   9   10   11   12

Mathematical Thinking at Grade 1

More Spots

Circle the puppy on the right that has more spots than the puppy on the left.

1

2

3

Mixed Review and Test Prep

4 Which picture shows 5 crayons in all?

Ⓐ   Ⓑ   Ⓒ   Ⓓ

Mathematical Thinking at Grade 1

Seven in All

Draw apples and bananas so that there are 7 pieces of fruit in all on each plate.

Family Connection

Students have been identifying different combinations of 7 (1 and 6, 2 and 5, and so on). To make combinations of 7, your child may want to count real objects, draw pictures, or use his or her knowledge of number combinations. You may wish to encourage your child to draw more plates on a sheet of paper and find more combinations.

1

2

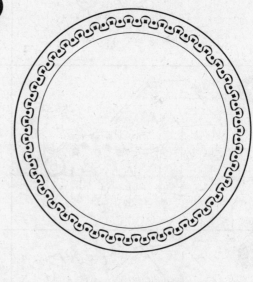

3

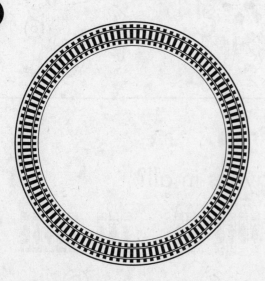

4

Name _____ Date _____

Mathematical Thinking at Grade 1

Order, Please!

1 Write the numbers to put the cards in order. Then connect the towers of cubes to the right number.

Family Connection

Students have been building "staircases" with 1 to 12 cubes making up each step, and labeling each step with a number card to tell how many cubes make up that step. You may wish to help your child cut out paper squares to represent cubes so he or she can "build" a staircase to show you.

| 11 | 9 | 6 | 3 | 8 | 1 | 12 | 2 | 5 | 10 | 4 | 7 |

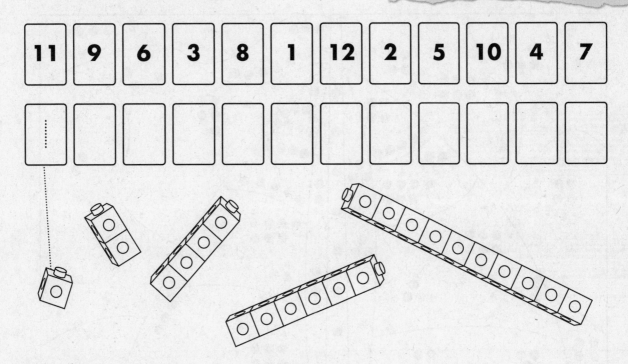

Mixed Review and Test Prep

2 Which basket has the same number of books in it?

Ⓐ

Ⓑ

Ⓒ

Ⓓ

© Pearson Education, Inc. 1

Use during Investigation 2 (Exploring Numbers), Sessions 5 and 6.

9

Name   Date

Nine Is the Number

Color **only** the parts that show 9 dots.

Family Connection

Students have been finding combinations of 9, determining how many different ways peas and carrots can be added together so that there are 9 "things" (vegetables) altogether (7 and 2, 3 and 6, and so on). To help your child keep track of the number of dots in each dotted section, have him or her mark each dot while counting. You may also wish to discuss some of the combinations—and configurations—of dots that make 9 dots in all.

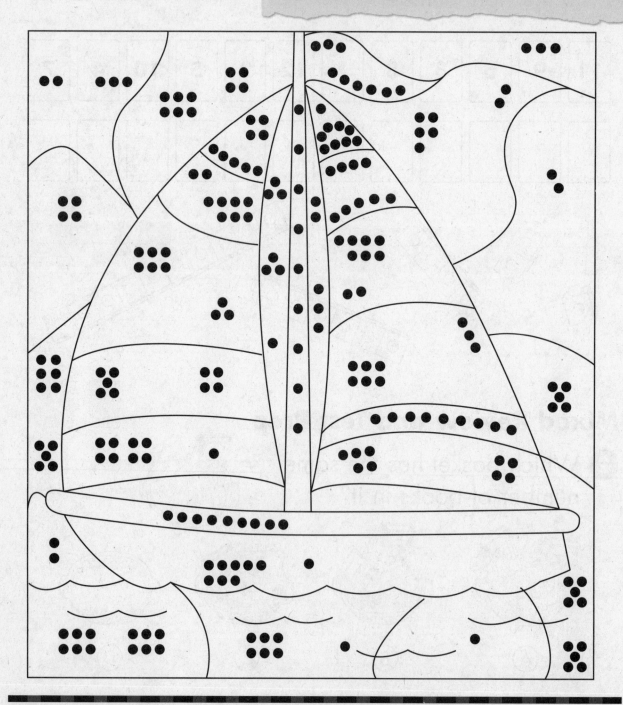

Mathematical Thinking at Grade 1

And the Next Square Is ...

Circle the square that shows what comes next.

Family Connection
Students have been playing a game called **What Comes Next?** in which they predict the color of the next cube in a pattern of interlocking cubes. After your child predicts what comes next, have him or her describe each pattern by naming the color sequence. (In Exercise 1, the pattern is white, gray; white, gray—a simple a-b-a-b pattern in which the basic pattern unit [the part that repeats] consists of two elements.)

1

2

3

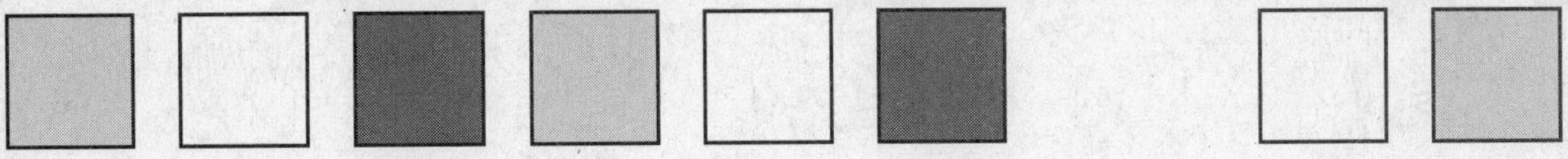

4

5

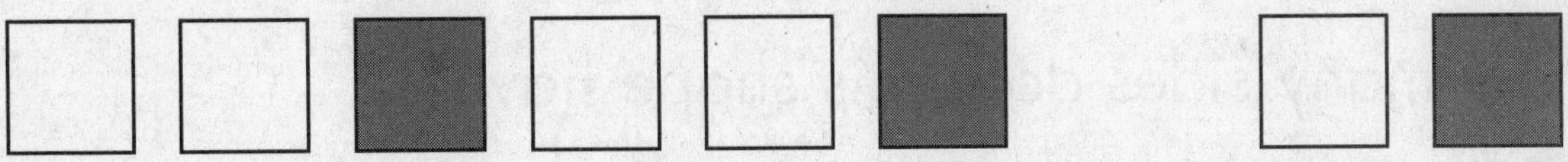

6

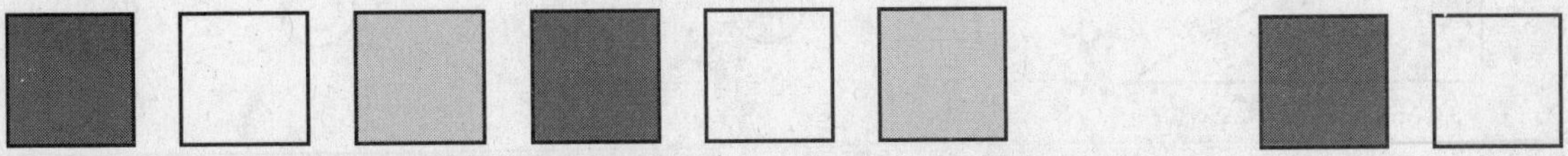

Show Me the Pattern!

Color the squares to show the pattern.

Family Connection

Students have been acting out sound and rhythm patterns using movements such as clap, clap, tap knees; clap, clap, tap knees. They are also learning how to represent each kind of pattern in another way. For example, clap, clap, tap knees; clap, clap, tap knees can be represented or translated using cubes in two colors, such as red, red, green; red, red, green.

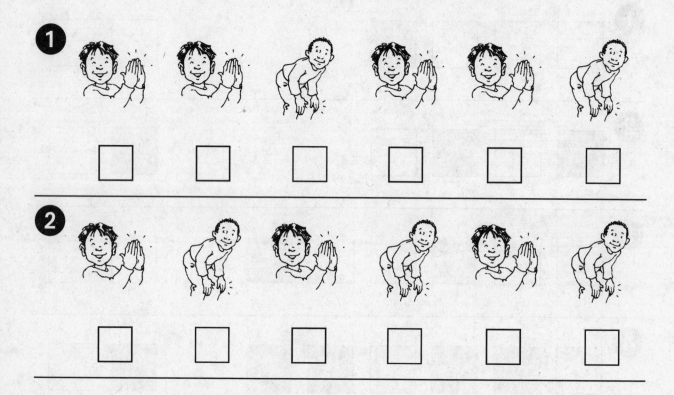

1

☐ ☐ ☐ ☐ ☐ ☐

2

☐ ☐ ☐ ☐ ☐ ☐

Mixed Review and Test Prep

How many sides does this shape have?

3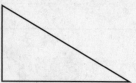

     0   1   2   3

    Ⓐ   Ⓑ   Ⓒ   Ⓓ

Mathematical Thinking at Grade 1

Match the Pattern

Use other colors to show the pattern.

Family Connection

Students have been comparing linear patterns and identifying how they are alike and how they are different. You may want to have your child create a pattern similar to ones shown on this page using materials at home. For example, a spoon, fork; spoon, fork (a-b-a-b) pattern is the same as the pattern shown in Exercise 1. Over time, children move from thinking about only which single element comes next to thinking about what the basic pattern unit (for example, spoon, fork) is—and where it first begins to repeat.

1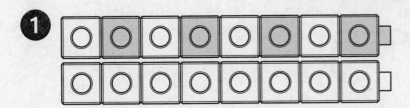

2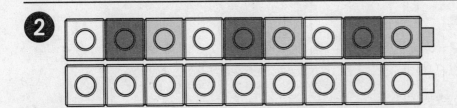

3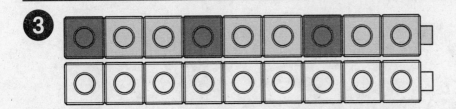

4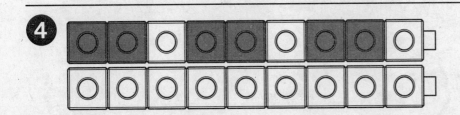

5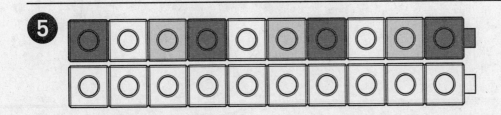

Go on a Pattern Hunt

Circle all the patterns you can find.

Family Connection

Students have been looking for patterns in the world around them as they become more aware of regularity and repetition. Have your child look for patterns at home and describe any patterns that he or she finds. Remind your child that not all patterns are linear sequences. Look for examples of patterns that might repeat in more than one direction (floor tiles) or patterns that might be built out from the center (quilts).

Mathematical Thinking at Grade 1

What Comes Next?

Draw the shape that comes next.

Family Connection

Students have used pattern blocks (geometric shapes) to make patterns. Then a partner has predicted which block comes next in the sequence. Have your child identify which two patterns are the same on this page. (Exercises 1 and 3 show the same pattern: a-b-b-a-b-b).

Mixed Review and Test Prep

5 How many children like bananas?

4	12	15	19
Ⓐ	Ⓑ	Ⓒ	Ⓓ

6 How many children do **not** like bananas?

19	15	5	4
Ⓐ	Ⓑ	Ⓒ	Ⓓ

Do you like bananas?

No	Yes

Mathematical Thinking at Grade 1

Match the Quilts

Match the quilts with the same pattern.

1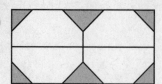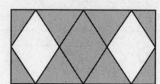

2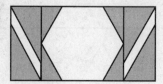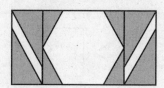

3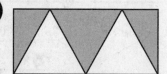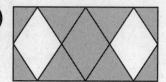

4 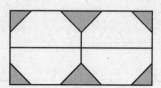

Mixed Review and Test Prep

5 How many eyes?

2   10   12   20

Ⓐ   Ⓑ   Ⓒ   Ⓓ

6 How many noses?

10   7   6   3

Ⓐ   Ⓑ   Ⓒ   Ⓓ

Mathematical Thinking at Grade 1

How Many Counters?

Stop working when
Jill and Ted have
collected 15 together.

Family Connection
Students played **Collect 15 Together.** The goal is for pairs to work together to collect at least 15 counters. Have your child follow the game that Jill and Ted are playing. Your child will count the dots, draw that many counters, and write how many there are in all.

	Draw counters.	How many in all?
1 Jill rolled ⚄ .	○ ○ ○ ○ ○	5
2 Ted rolled ⚂ .		___
3 Jill rolled ⚀ .		___
4 Ted rolled .		___
5 Jill rolled ⚃ .		___

Name _____ Date _____

Finish the Pattern

Color to complete the pattern on each blanket.

Family Connection

Students have been using objects to create linear repeating patterns—and then covering a portion of their patterns with paper, leaving only the first 2 or 3 objects showing. Partners then take turns trying to predict each other's sequence, one object at a time. You may wish to create a pattern using household items and have your child predict what comes next.

1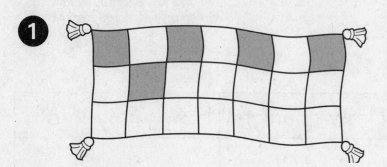

2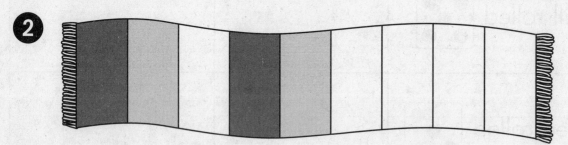

3 Draw your own blanket with a pattern!

Mixed Review and Test Prep

4 How many balls are in the jar?

3   4   5   6
Ⓐ   Ⓑ   Ⓒ   Ⓓ

Use during Investigation 4 (Counting and Combining), Sessions 2 and 3.

Mathematical Thinking at Grade 1

Compare Numbers

Circle the card that shows the greater number.

Family Connection

Students have been comparing two numbers and identifying which is greater. They also have been determining which of two totals is greater. You may wish to ask your child how he or she determines which number or total is greater. Does he "just know"? Does she start counting with 1, or count on from the greater number? Is he beginning to reason about number combinations?

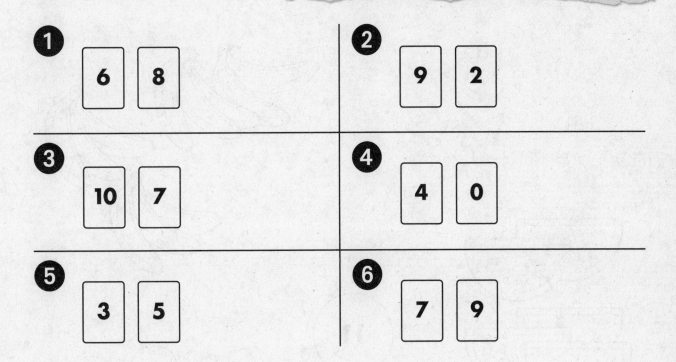

1 6 8

2 9 2

3 10 7

4 4 0

5 3 5

6 7 9

Circle the **pair** of cards that shows the greater total.

7 2 8   5 7

8 6 2   4 3

9 7 8   9 5

10 4 4   0 9

Mathematical Thinking at Grade 1

Find Eleven Pieces of Fruit

Draw a line from the number 11 to each group that shows 11 pieces of fruit.

Family Connection
Students have been working on finding combinations of 11 (3 and 8, 5 and 6, and so on). You may wish to ask your child if he or she thinks all of the combinations of 11 are shown on this page and to explain his or her reasoning.

Name _____ Date _____

What's Next?

Draw what you think comes next.

1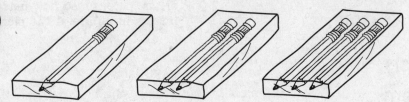

2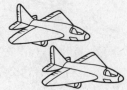

3

Mixed Review and Test Prep

4 How many triangles?

6   5   4   3

Ⓐ   Ⓑ   Ⓒ   Ⓓ

5 How many circles?

2   3   5   6

Ⓐ   Ⓑ   Ⓒ   Ⓓ

Where Is Everybody?

These insects are at the picnic:
1 beetle, 2 mosquitoes,
3 grasshoppers, 4 butterflies,
5 ladybugs, and 6 ants.

1 Find the insects
and circle them.

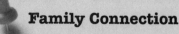

Family Connection

Students have been solving problems that ask how many things there are in all. Students count, use patterns, draw pictures, and use other strategies to help solve the problems. You may wish to ask your child how he or she determined how many insects in all are at the picnic.

2 How many insects in all are at the picnic? _____

Mixed Review and Test Prep

3 What is 4 and 4?

    9   8   7   5

    Ⓐ   Ⓑ   Ⓒ   Ⓓ

Mathematical Thinking at Grade 1

How Many?

1 How many students do you count? _____

Family Connection

Students counted the number of children in their class today. Then they made "Kid Pins," each using a clothespin and a flat stick with his or her name on it. Students will use the pins throughout this investigation (and later in the year) to take attendance and to answer survey questions.

2 How many students do you count? _____

Mixed Review and Test Prep

3 How many cubes high is step A?

  2   3   5   7

  Ⓐ   Ⓑ   Ⓒ   Ⓓ

4 How many cubes high is step B?

  7   6   4   3

  Ⓐ   Ⓑ   Ⓒ   Ⓓ

Two Surveys

Do you have a pet?

Family Connection

Students have been taking surveys, recording the results, and discussing what they have learned from the data. This page shows the results of two surveys. You may wish to ask your child to explain how he or she used the survey data to answer the questions.

1 How many students have pets? _____

2 How many students do **not** have pets? _____

3 How many students are there in all? _____

Are you wearing red?

4 How many students are wearing red? _____

5 How many students are **not** wearing red? _____

6 How many students are there in all? _____

Show It Another Way

Match the Attendance Surveys
with the Kid Pin boards.

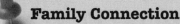

Family Connection

Students have been discussing and
interpreting results of surveys and
learning that there are different
ways to show the same thing.
You may wish to talk with your
child about how representations
of the data on this page are the
same and how they are different.

Attendance Surveys

Who's here?
October 1

17 here, 4 absent
21 total

Who's here?
October 8

20 here, 1 absent
21 total

Who's here?
October 15

15 here, 6 absent
21 total

Who's here?
October 22

16 here, 5 absent
21 total

Kid Pin Boards

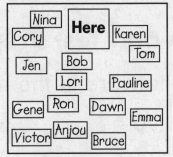

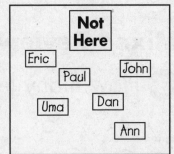

Use during Investigation 5 (Data About Our Class), Sessions 3 and 4.

25

Mathematical Thinking at Grade 1

Recording Results

Do you like oranges?
yes yes no no yes no
no no no yes no yes
yes yes no no yes yes
no no no no yes

Family Connection
Students have partici-
pated in surveys and then
made their own representations of the data using pictures, numbers, words, and
concrete materials. As your
child is working on this
page, ask him or her what
the categories are (likes
oranges, does not like
oranges) and how many
people are in each category
(10 and 13, respectively).

Mr. Black's class took a survey.

1 Draw ☺ to show each student who likes oranges.

2 Draw ☹ to show each student who does **not** like oranges.

Mixed Review and Test Prep

3 How many letters are in the name **Kwan**?

   4   5   6   7

  Ⓐ   Ⓑ   Ⓒ   Ⓓ

4 How many letters are in the name **Thomas**?

   7   6   5   4

  Ⓐ   Ⓑ   Ⓒ   Ⓓ

Use after Investigation 5 (Data About Our Class), Sessions 3 and 4.

Showing Data

Students in Ms. Smith's class took a survey about favorite foods. Complete the chart to show this information:

> **Family Connection**
> Students have been collecting and analyzing data having more than two categories. (In this survey, the categories are tacos, spaghetti, and pizza.) You might suggest that your child show the information in this survey by writing the students' names, by drawing pictures, or by using tally marks to indicate each person's favorite food in the appropriate column.

1 Mary, Berto, and Alex like tacos best.

2 Sumi, Ben, Abby, Marco, Tina, and Niko like spaghetti best.

3 Forest, Kellin, Rachel, Lauren, Taylor, Sam, and Olivia like pizza best.

Our Favorite Foods		
Tacos	Spaghetti	Pizza

Mixed Review and Test Prep

4 What is the total of the two number cards?

3	6

   3   6   9   12

  Ⓐ   Ⓑ   Ⓒ   Ⓓ

Mathematical Thinking at Grade 1

What Does It Show?

This is Max's drawing. It shows how students in his class get to school.

Family Connection

Students have been discussing their representations of data about how their classmates get to school. You may wish to ask your child how the representation shown on this page is similar to or different from what your child found out about how students in his or her class get to school.

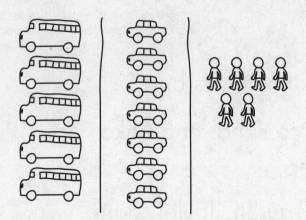

Interesting Tidbit

Of every 100 school children in the United States, only 13 walk to school!

1 Circle the pictures that show how students get to school.

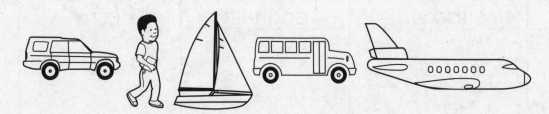

2 How many students get to school by bus? _____

3 How many students get to school by car? _____

4 How many students walk to school? _____

5 How many students are in Max's class? _____

6 On another sheet of paper, draw a picture that shows how you get to school.

Building Number Sense

I See Dots!

Draw a line to match the sentence to the correct dot card.

1 I see 5 dots.

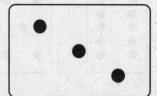

2 I see 3 dots.

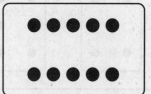

3 I see 10 dots.

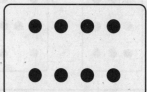

4 I see 8 dots.

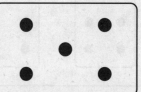

5 I see 6 dots.

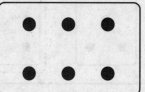

Name _____   Date _____

Building Number Sense

Which Has More?

Circle the card that has **more** dots.

Family Connection

Students have been playing a game called **Compare Dots** in which they determine which of two dot patterns has more dots. Ask your child to explain how he or she knows which dot card has more dots. Then, for each pair of cards, have your child tell you which dot card has fewer dots.

1

2

3

4

5

6

7

8

9

10

30 *Use after Investigation 1 (Visualizing Numbers), Session 2.*

© Pearson Education, Inc. **1**

Building Number Sense

How Many Cubes?

Write how many cubes are in each model in the top row. Then draw a line to the matching model in the bottom row.

(HINT: The colors do not have to match.)

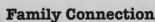
Family Connection

Students have been using interlocking cubes to build objects (arrangements of cubes) that match given objects and then counting the number of cubes in each object they have built. Make sure your child matches the objects that are the same and records how many cubes are in each object.

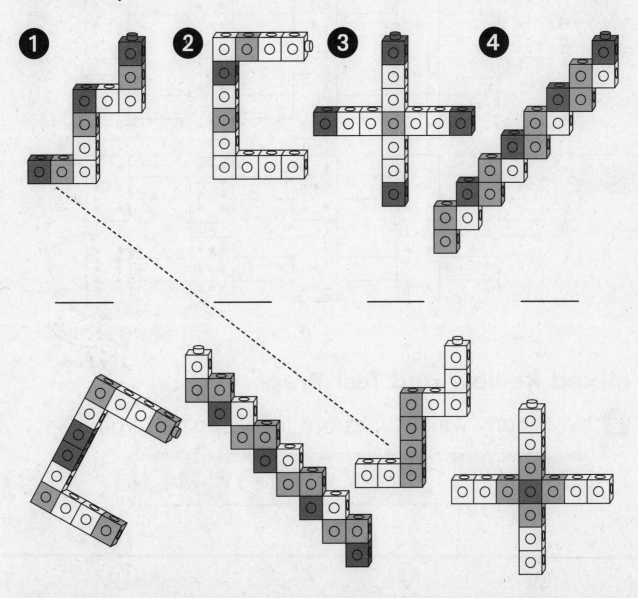

Building Number Sense

This Frog Needs Help!

1 The frog has to hop from one dot card to the nearest dot card that shows **more** dots. Draw a line to show his path to the lily pad.

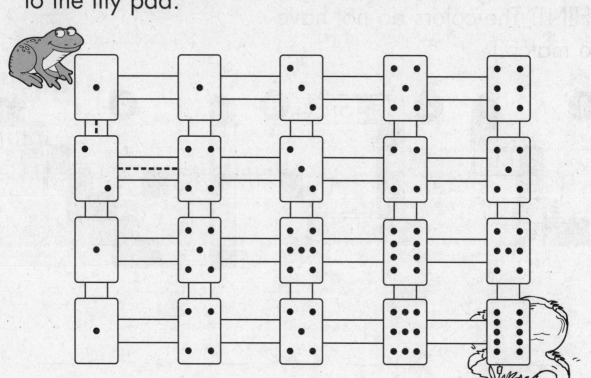

Lily Pad

Mixed Review and Test Prep

2 How many white cubes are in this pattern train?

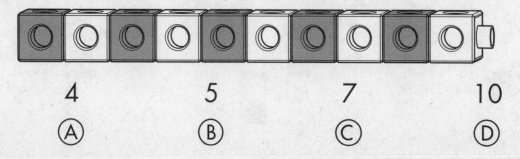

4   5   7   10

Ⓐ   Ⓑ   Ⓒ   Ⓓ

Name _____   Date _____

How Many Dots?

Write the number
that tells how
many dots.

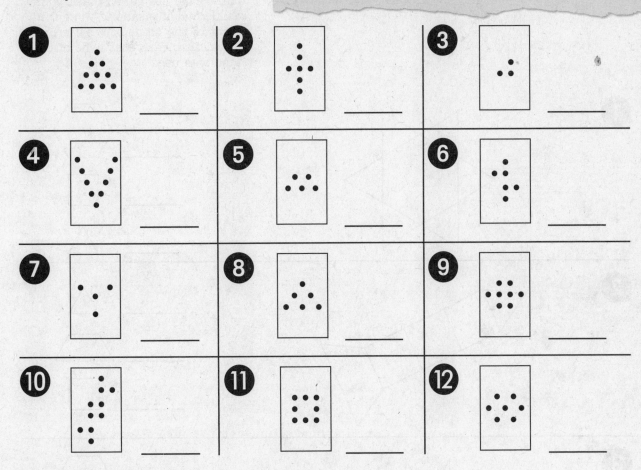

1 _____

2 _____

3 _____

4 _____

5 _____

6 _____

7 _____

8 _____

9 _____

10 _____

11 _____

12 _____

Mixed Review and Test Prep

13 Which shows 4 cubes?

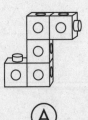 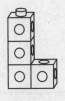

Name _____   Date _____

Building Number Sense

Counting Pattern Blocks

Look at each design.
Write the number of each kind
of pattern block in the design.

Family Connection

Students have been making
designs with pattern blocks and
then counting each kind of pattern
block to determine how many of
that kind of block were used in the
design. Ask your child how many
pattern blocks in all were used to
make each design. Also ask your
child what it means to write 0 in
front of the name of a pattern-
block. (It means that none of that
kind was used.)

1

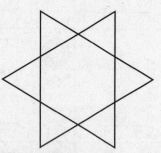

_____ ⬡

_____ ▢

_____ △

2

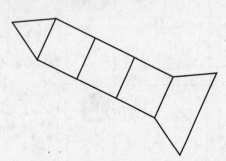

_____ △

_____ ⬟

_____ ▢

3

_____ ⬡

_____ ⬟

_____ △

_____ ▱

34

Use after Investigation 1 (Visualizing Numbers), Sessions 5 and 6.

Name _____   Date _____

Building Number Sense

Make a Dot Picture

1 Circle the dot pictures that you think are easiest to remember.

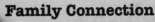

Family Connection

Students have been looking at dot images and are finding ways to organize sets of dots so that they are easy to count. You may wish to ask your child what makes some dot images more difficult to count than others and how he or she would reorganize the dots to make them easier to count.

 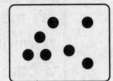  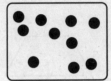

Draw each number of dots in a way that is easy to remember.

2 Show 7 dots.

3 Show 10 dots.

4 Show 5 dots.

5 Show 8 dots.

Mixed Review and Test Prep

6 Which cube tower shows 6?

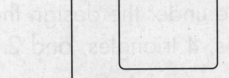

Ⓐ   Ⓑ   Ⓒ   Ⓓ

© Pearson Education, Inc. 1

Use during Investigation 1 (Visualizing Numbers), Sessions 7 and 8.

35

Building Number Sense

I Spy Pattern Blocks

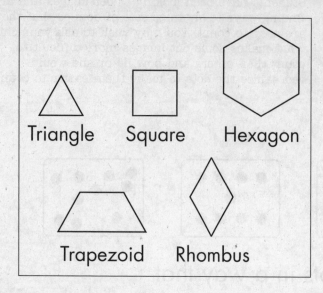

Triangle   Square   Hexagon

Trapezoid   Rhombus

Family Connection

Students have been creating designs using pattern blocks and recording the number of each kind of block. Ask your child to tell you which design on this page uses the most blocks.

Interesting Tidbit

Tri means "having 3." A **tri**angle has 3 sides and 3 corners. A **tri**cycle has 3 wheels.

1 Circle the design that uses 4 triangles, 2 rhombuses, and 2 squares.

2 Draw a line under the design that uses 3 hexagons, 4 triangles, and 2 trapezoids.

3 Draw a box around the design that uses 9 triangles, 0 squares, and 2 trapezoids.

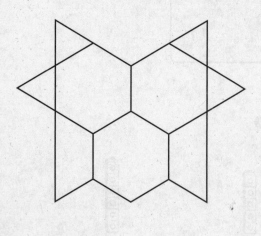
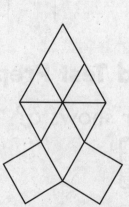
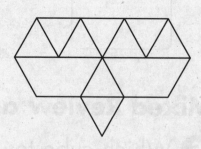

Name _____   Date _____

Dots, Dots, and More Dots

Draw another way to show the same number of dots.

1

2

3

4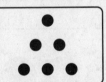

5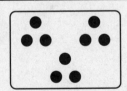

Mixed Review and Test Prep

6 How many shoes are the same?

7   5   4   2

Ⓐ   Ⓑ   Ⓒ   Ⓓ

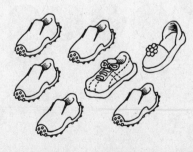

© Pearson Education, Inc. **1**

Name _____   Date _____

12 in All

Draw more counters
to show 12 in all.

Family Connection

Students have been finding combinations of two
numbers that make 12 (5 and 7, 3 and 9, and so on).
This activity helps students develop their understanding of number relationships and of strategies for
combining quantities. Ask your child to tell you how
he or she determined how many more counters were
needed to show 12 in all.

1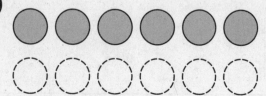

2

3

4

5

6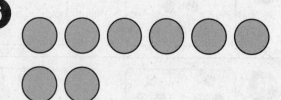

7

8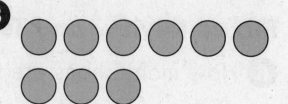

Name _____ Date _____

The Total Is 10

Draw a line to match boys and girls so that there are 10 children in all.

Family Connection

Students have been creating and solving problems in which there are 10 things in all. First they decide on 2 kinds of things, such as apples and oranges. Then (using apples and oranges as an example) they decide how many of each kind of fruit there can be so that the total number of pieces is 10.

Mixed Review and Test Prep

6 How many cars are shown?

6   7   8   9

Ⓐ   Ⓑ   Ⓒ   Ⓓ

Name _____ Date _____

Building Number Sense

Which Is Larger?

Circle the pair of numbers that makes the larger total.

Family Connection

Students have been playing the game **Double Compare.** Using pairs of number cards, they find which of two totals is the greater. Ask your child how he or she knows which pair of number cards makes the greater total in each exercise.

1    3 8   6 2

2 5 5   10 3

3 9 4   1 7

4 2 8   7 9

5 6 6   4 10

6 5 2   3 1

7 7 8   9 2

8 1 6   2 2

9 4 8   10 7

10 5 1   9 3

Name

Date

Building Number Sense

How Many Apples?

There were 7 apples on each tree, but some fell off. Write how many apples are still on the tree and how many fell off.

Family Connection

Students played a new game, **On and Off,** in which they tossed a set of counters over a piece of paper and recorded how many counters landed on the paper and how many landed off the paper. After your child has completed this page, ask him or her whether there are any other combinations of 7 that are not shown here.

 1

On _____ Off _____

2

On _____ Off _____

3

On _____ Off _____

4

On _____ Off _____

5

On _____ Off _____

6

On _____ Off _____

Building Number Sense

What's in the Bag?

There are 5 balls in all. Write how many balls are **outside** the bag. Write how many balls are **inside** the bag.

Family Connection

Students have been playing **Counters in a Cup.** In this game they find combinations of 5 (1 and 4, 2 and 3, and so on). You might ask your child to determine how many balls might be in and out of the bag if there were 6, 7, or 8 balls in all.

1   Outside _____

Inside _____

2   Outside _____

Inside _____

3   Outside _____

Inside _____

4   Outside _____

Inside _____

Mixed Review and Test Prep

5 How many of these shapes have 4 sides?

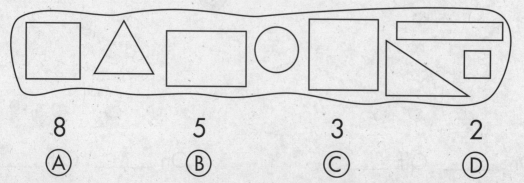

8   5   3   2

Ⓐ   Ⓑ   Ⓒ   Ⓓ

Building Number Sense

Looking at Towers

Look at each tower of 10.
Write how many white cubes.
Write how many gray cubes.

1

_____ white

_____ gray

2

_____ white

_____ gray

3

_____ white

_____ gray

4

_____ white

_____ gray

5

_____ white

_____ gray

6

_____ white

_____ gray

Name _____ Date _____

Building Number Sense

What's Inside the Cup?

There are 9 counters in all.
Write how many counters are
outside the cup. Write how many
counters are **inside** the cup.

Family Connection
Students continue to find
combinations of numbers. Ask
your child to explain how he or
she decides how many counters
are under each cup.

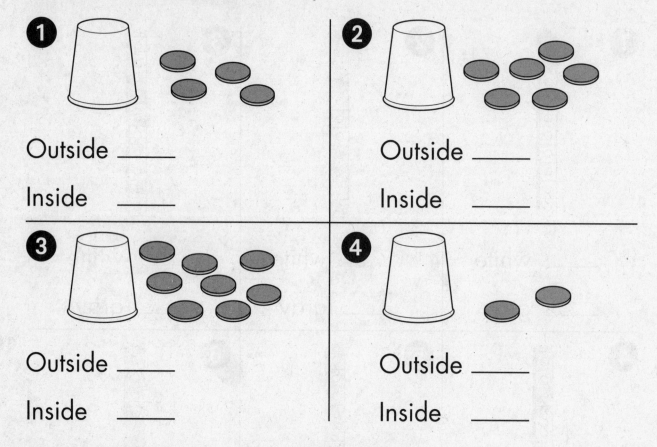

1
Outside _____
Inside _____

2
Outside _____
Inside _____

3
Outside _____
Inside _____

4
Outside _____
Inside _____

Mixed Review and Test Prep

5 Which pair of number cards has a total of 7?

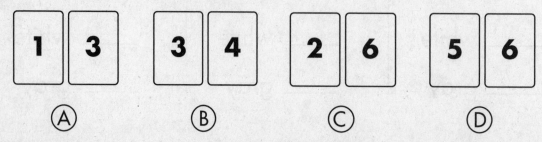

1 3	3 4	2 6	5 6
Ⓐ	Ⓑ	Ⓒ	Ⓓ

© Pearson Education, Inc. 1

Building Number Sense

Trains and Towers

Color each cube train and tower to show a different combination of 10. Then record the combination.

Family Connection

Students have been sharing the combinations of 10 that they got while playing **Towers of 10.** Ask your child to record any combination for 10 that is not on this page using pictures, numbers, words, or number expressions.

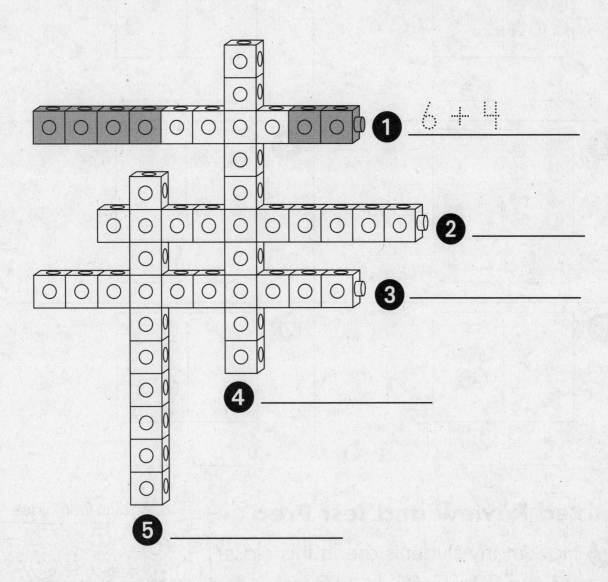

1 6 + 4 _____

2 _____

3 _____

4 _____

5 _____

15 Is the Number

Draw dots so there are 15 in all. Write how many dots in each part.

1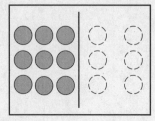

    9   6

2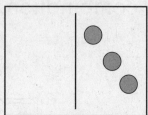

    ___ ___

3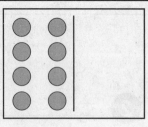

    ___ ___

4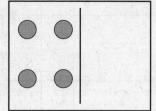

    ___ ___

5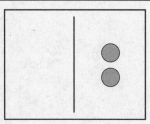

    ___ ___

6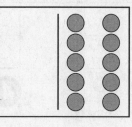

    ___ ___

Mixed Review and Test Prep

Students in Our Class

7 How many students are in this class?

24   22   21   19
Ⓐ   Ⓑ   Ⓒ   Ⓓ

Building Number Sense

Missing Numbers

Circle 5, 8, 14, and 19.

Family Connection

Students have been exploring number patterns on the 100 chart. They are also learning to read and write numbers sequentially. You may wish to cover several numbers in each exercise and ask your child to tell you which numbers are missing.

1

1	2	3	4	5	6	7	8	9	10
11	12	13	14	15	16	17	18	19	20

Fill in the missing numbers.

2

1		3		5		7		9	
11		13		15		17		19	

3

	2		4		6		8		10
	12		14		16		18		20

4

21		23	24			27	28		30
	32	33	34	35			38	39	

5

	22	23		25	26			29	30
31		33			36	37			40

Building Number Sense

Keep Counting

Fill in the missing numbers on the counting strips.

Family Connection

Students have been making counting strips. They begin with the number 1 and write numbers, one under the other, as high as they can count. Make sure your child understands that the counting strips in Exercises 3 and 4 are partial number strips and that the beginning part of each strip is not visible.

1

1
2
3
4

2

1
2

3

4
6

4

8
11

Mixed Review and Test Prep

5 How many boys are in this class?

Ⓐ 5

Ⓑ 12

Ⓒ 15

Ⓓ 17

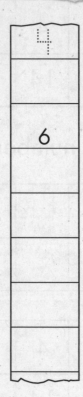
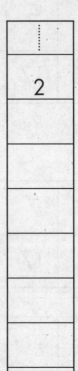

Today's Question: Are you a boy or a girl?

girl

Ann	Carol
Lina	Jessica
Pamela	Hillary
Tichina	Andrea
Melin	Drew
Joan	Sayaka
Ingrid	Kim
Becky	

boy

Rashid	Frank
Brandon	Victor
Evan	Takiro
Joshua	Reuben
Ryan	Vladimir
Mitchel	Cory
Jackson	Raymond
Russel	Vipin
	Marcek

Name _____   Date _____

Which Holds More Cubes?

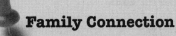

Family Connection
Students have been estimating which of two containers holds more cubes. In this unit, the emphasis is on counting and comparing numbers. In a later unit, a similar activity will focus on capacity.

32   **18**   **21**   **13**   **40**

  A   B   C   D   E

Write the letter of the container that holds more.

1 Which container holds more, A or B? _____

2 Which container holds more, B or C? _____

3 Which container holds more, D or E? _____

4 Which container holds more, A or E? _____

5 Which container holds more, C or D? _____

Name _____   Date _____

Number Riddles

Solve each riddle.

Family Connection

Students are continuing to locate numbers on the 100 chart and explore patterns in the number sequence. You may wish to help your child write number riddles for family members to solve.

1 I come after 10.
I come before 12.

I am _____.

2 I come after 20.
I come before 22.

I am _____.

3 I come after 29.
I come before 31.

I am _____.

4 I have a 2 and a 6.
I come after 30.

I am _____.

5 I have a 3 and a 7.
I come before 40.

I am _____.

6 I am between 1 and 100.
I am 1 away from 100.

I am _____.

A 100 chart can help me solve number riddles!

1	2	3	4	5	6	7	8	9	10
11	12	13	14	15	16	17	18	19	20
21	22	23	24	25	26	27	28	29	30
31	32	33	34	35	36	37	38	39	40
41	42	43	44	45	46	47	48	49	50
51	52	53	54	55	56	57	58	59	60
61	62	63	64	65	66	67	68	69	70
71	72	73	74	75	76	77	78	79	80
81	82	83	84	85	86	87	88	89	90
91	92	93	94	95	96	97	98	99	100

Building Number Sense

Number Patterns

Complete the 100 chart.
Look for patterns.

Family Connection

Students are continuing to discover number patterns as they work with the 100 chart—number patterns that reveal the structure of the number system.

	2	3	4		6	7	8	9	
11		13	14		16	17	18		20
21	22		24		26	27		29	30
31	32	33			36		38	39	40
						47	48	49	50
51	52	53	54						
61	62	63		65			68	69	70
71	72		74	75		77		79	80
81		83	84	85		87	88		90
	92	93	94	95		97	98	99	

Building Number Sense

Roll and Roll Again

Complete each sentence.

> **Family Connection**
>
> After your child completes this page about number combinations, you may wish to play **Ten Turns,** a game students are learning to play in class. Use a dot cube or a number cube and have your child accumulate pennies each time he or she rolls the cube: "I rolled 4 and then 2. I got 4 cents and then 2 cents. So now I have 6 cents." Do this ten times for a round of the game.

1 If I roll 4 and then 2, the total will be _____.

2 If I roll 2 and then 4, the total will be _____.

3 If I roll 3 and then 3, the total will be _____.

4 If I roll 5 and then 1, the total will be _____.

5 If I roll 1 and then 5, the total will be _____.

6 If I roll 1 and then 4, the total will be _____.

7 If I roll 1 and then 3, the total will be _____.

8 If I roll 1 and then 2, the total will be _____.

9 If I roll 1 and then 1, the total will be _____.

10 If I roll 4 and then 4, the total will be _____.

Mixed Review and Test Prep

11 How many cubes are there in all?

23   18   13   12

Ⓐ   Ⓑ   Ⓒ   Ⓓ

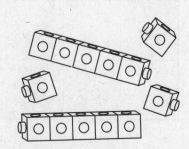

Building Number Sense

What Went Wrong?

Here are parts of 4 counting strips. Cross out each wrong number and write the correct number to fix the mistakes.

Family Connection

Throughout Investigation 3, students have been creating counting strips on which they write numbers from 1 to 100 (or higher, if they wish). Learning to correctly write numbers in sequence takes time. Many students have difficulty when crossing decades (from 19 to 20, from 29 to 30). Others get confused about the order of the digits and may write "21" when they mean to write "12."

1 | 11
12
~~14~~ 13
15
16

2 | 21
22
23
33
43

3 | 17
18
19
30
31

4 | 9
10
11
12
14

5 | 25
26
27
38
49

Mixed Review and Test Prep

6 How many children were surveyed?

7   12   16   22

Ⓐ   Ⓑ   Ⓒ   Ⓓ

Do you wear glasses?

Yes	No
IIII I	IIII IIII

Building Number Sense

All Kinds of Patterns

Color the boxes to make a **color** pattern that matches the **movement** pattern.

> **Family Connection**
> Students are learning that there are many different kinds of repeating patterns, including sound and movement patterns, color patterns, shape patterns, and number patterns. With practice, they learn to identify the pattern "unit" (the part that repeats) and to continue the pattern.

1

2

3

Mixed Review and Test Prep

4 Which pattern block has 6 sides?

Ⓐ   Ⓑ   Ⓒ   Ⓓ

How Many?

Count each group
of objects. Write
how many.

1

How many? _____

2

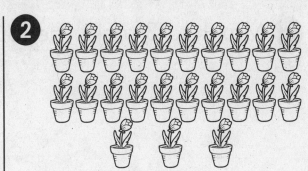

How many? _____

3

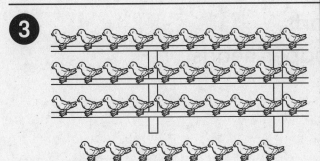

How many? _____

4

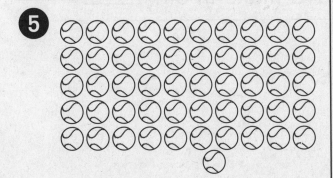

How many? _____

5

How many? _____

6

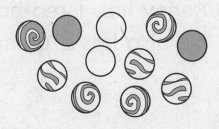

How many? _____

© Pearson Education, Inc. **1**

Combining Groups

Read the problem.
Show what happened.
Then solve the problem.

1 Max had 3 rocks. He found 2 more rocks.

How many rocks did Max have then? _____

2 Maya made 2 paper hearts.
Then she made 4 more paper hearts.

How many hearts did Maya make in all? _____

3 Kenny has 1 red ball.
He also has 2 green balls.

How many balls does Kenny have in all? _____

Building Number Sense

Separating Groups

Read the problem.
Show what happened.
Then solve the problem.

Family Connection

Students are solving separating problems in which they find the result when one quantity is removed from another. Similar to the way in which your child solves combining problems, he or she should focus on visualizing what happens in a separating kind of problem—and on deciding whether there will be more or less than the quantity he or she started with.

1 Kit had 7 balloons. 4 of them blew away.

How many balloons did Kit have left? _____

2 There were 12 apples in a bowl.
Kiyo put 2 of them on a plate.

How many apples were left in the bowl? _____

3 5 friends were playing soccer.
Then 2 went home.

How many children were left playing soccer? _____

Name _____   Date _____

What's the Sum?

Find the sum of the two numbers.

> **Family Connection**
> Students have been playing a game called **Five-in-a-Row** in which they toss number cubes and find the sum of the digits. If needed, provide counters your child can use to represent each number. Then your child can combine the counters to find the sum.

	What's the sum?
1 [6] [5]	_____
2 [2] [3]	_____
3 [8] [4]	_____
4 [1] [7]	_____

Mixed Review and Test Prep

5 Which pattern-block "snake" is made with 8 blocks?

  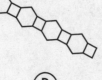 

Ⓐ   Ⓑ   Ⓒ   Ⓓ

Name _____ Date _____

How Did They Do That?

1 Look at Lin and Jamie's gameboard. Circle the pairs of numbers they used to make five-in-a-row.

Family Connection

Students continue to play **Five-in-a-Row.** On this page, students are shown a gameboard on which Lin and Jamie have already found 5 sums in a row. Ask your child to explain how he or she will determine which pairs of numbers have sums of 7, 9, 11, 6, and 2.

2	12	7	6	12
9	5	4	10	8
7	9	11	6	2
9	5	11	3	10
11	3	8	4	2

6 and 6   6 and 5

5 and 4   1 and 5

2 and 2   2 and 3

6 and 4   3 and 4

1 and 1   2 and 1

Mixed Review and Test Prep

2 Which cube train has more cubes than the tower on the right?

(A)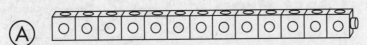

(B)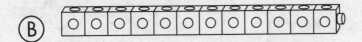

(C)

(D)

Name _____   Date _____

Two Story Problems

Solve each problem.
Show how you found
your answer.

Family Connection

Students are solving more story problems. Remind your child to first decide whether the quantities are being combined or separated. **Questions you might ask your child:** "How does the problem start? What happens next? Do you end up with more or less than what you started with?" Ask your child to explain how he or she solved each problem.

1 Jill had 4 fish. She got 5 more for her birthday. How many fish did Jill have then? _____

2 Myles had 15 stamps in his collection. He gave 5 of them to his brother. How many stamps did Myles have left? _____

Mixed Review and Test Prep

3 Which group has the same number of objects as keys?

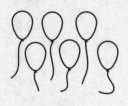
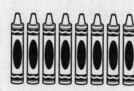

 Ⓐ   Ⓑ   Ⓒ   Ⓓ

Name _____   Date _____

Building Number Sense

Fill in the Dots

Draw dots on the cards to make each number. Use only the dot cards shown.

1 Make 6.

2 Make 7.

3 Make 9.

4 Make 11.

5 Make 14.

Use after Investigation 4 (Addition and Subtraction), Session 6.   **61**

Family Connection

Students have been playing **Dot Addition.** Pairs of students get a set of dot cards having 2 to 5 dots per card. The object of the game is to combine dot cards to make given numbers. On this page, your child is given a specific number of cards and must determine a combination of dot cards that makes the given number.

© Pearson Education, Inc. **1**

Building Number Sense

Adding Dots

Write how many dots in all.

Family Connection

In today's version of the Quick Images routine, students were shown combinations of two or three of the same cards, with up to 5 dots per card. Ask your child to try to quickly identify how many dots there are in each exercise and then to explain how he or she determines the total.

1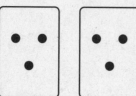

_____

2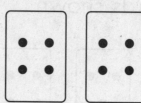

_____

3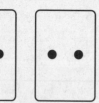

_____

4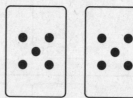

_____

5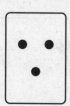

_____

6

_____

7

_____

8

_____

Name _____ Date _____

More Story Problems

Solve each problem.
Record your work.
Show how you found
your answer.

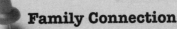

Family Connection

Students are continuing to solve story problems.
Ask your child how he or she found the answer to
each problem. Is he or she counting each quantity
by 1's? Counting up or counting down from one
number to the other? Or does your child "just
know" some of the number combinations?

1 Rick has 12 shells. He
finds 3 more. How
many shells does he
have now? _____

2 There are 10 lizards
on the rocks. 6 of the
lizards run away. How
many lizards are still
on the rocks? _____

Mixed Review and Test Prep

3 There should be 8 crayons in the
box. How many more are needed?

Name _____ Date _____

Draw It, Write It

Draw dots on the cards to make each number. Use only the dot cards shown. Write the addition combination.

1 Make 6. $3 + 3$

2 Make 12.

3 Make 9.

4 Make 8.

Mixed Review and Test Prep

5 How many pattern blocks are in this design?

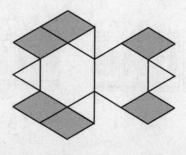

8	9	10	12
Ⓐ	Ⓑ	Ⓒ	Ⓓ

Use after Investigation 4 (Addition and Subtraction), Sessions 7, 8, and 9.

Name _____   Date _____

Show the Same Patterns

Use ◯, △, and ☐ to make patterns like the ones shown.

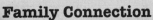

Family Connection

As an assessment, students solved story problems and recorded their solutions. Then students acted out repeating clapping patterns. On this page, your child is given color patterns and is asked to represent the same patterns using shapes. Your child can also represent the patterns using physical actions, objects, pictures, and numbers.

1
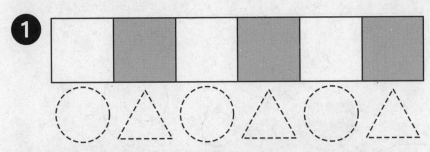

2
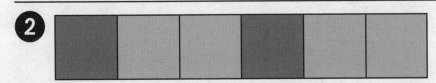

3
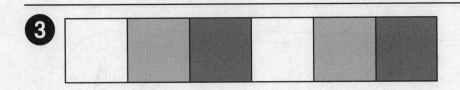

4
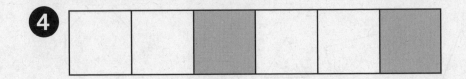

Name _____   Date _____

What's My Rule?

Draw a line to each shape that fits the rule.

Family Connection

Students have been exploring attribute blocks and describing what makes them alike and different, focusing on color, shape, size, and thickness. Students also played a game in which the teacher made up a "secret sorting rule" and then placed blocks that followed the rule together into a set. Students then looked at the blocks to see what they had in common so they could determine the rule according to which blocks had been sorted.

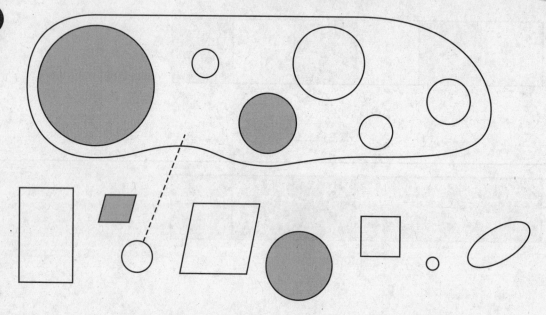

Use during Investigation 1 (Sorting), Sessions 1 and 2.

Show Me the Rule!

Draw another shape that follows the rule. Then complete the sentence.

1

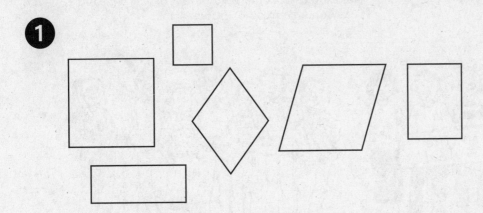

The secret rule is _____.

2

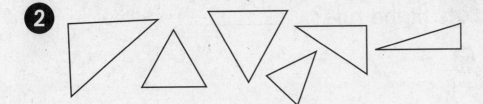

The secret rule is _____.

Mixed Review and Test Prep

3 How many tiles are in this border?

29	28	25	20
Ⓐ	Ⓑ	Ⓒ	Ⓓ

Name _____   Date _____

Survey Questions and Secret Rules

Two Groups

Look at the two groups.
What secret rule did
the teacher use to sort
the students?

Family Connection

In class, students were sorted according to an
obvious attribute, such as clothing color, and then
took turns suggesting someone else that might fit
the "secret rule." If a person didn't fit the rule,
students were asked to think about how that
person was different from those who did fit the rule.
Students discovered that both positive examples
(in this case, people who fit the rule) and negative
examples (people who didn't fit the rule) are
valuable sources of information.

1 Does fit the rule? _____

2 Does fit the rule? _____

3 Does  fit the rule? _____

4 Does  fit the rule? _____

5 The secret rule is _____.

68 *Use after Investigation 1 (Sorting), Session 3.*

© Pearson Education, Inc. 1

This Button Belongs Here

Match each button in the box to the right group. Then match each group to the right rule!

Family Connection

Students have been talking about the attributes of a collection of buttons. They also played **Guess My Rule with Buttons,** a game in which they look at a group of buttons and try to identify another button that belongs in that group. Ask your child to explain how he or she is deciding which button belongs in each group and which sorting rule each group follows.

Dark Buttons

Square Buttons

Buttons with 2 Holes

Small Buttons

Looking at Lids

Circle the lids that fit the rule.

Family Connection
Today students compared container lids, discussing how they were the same and how they were different. Then students were presented with a group of lids that fit a rule, and had to find other lids that also fit the rule. You may want to ask your child to compare lids that he or she finds at home, discussing how they are the same and how they are different.

1 Lids with Words

2 Lids with Pictures

3 Lids That Are About the Same Size

4 Big Lids

5 Lids with Numbers

Do You Know the Rule?

Write the rule that tells how the buttons are sorted.

Family Connection
Students have been sorting lids and buttons, making representations of their sortings, and then writing the sorting rules on small pieces of paper. They attached the papers, facedown, to their representations so that the rules could not be seen. Students then played **Guess My Rule** with one another. You may wish to ask your child to draw a button that fits the rule in each of the first three exercises.

1

The secret rule is _____.

2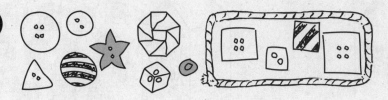

The secret rule is _____.

3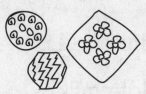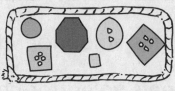

The secret rule is _____.

Mixed Review and Test Prep

4 Which group shows **one more** than the number of marbles?

Ⓐ   Ⓑ   Ⓒ   Ⓓ

Would You Rather ...?

"Would you rather drink white milk or chocolate milk?"

Students answered this question by putting a cube next to the white milk carton or the chocolate milk carton.

Family Connection

In the previous investigation, students sorted objects that could be moved around, such as buttons, lids, and even people. In this investigation, students sort people by what they **think** or **do.** Students learned that they can take surveys to find out what people think and then organize the results in a way that tells the story of the data.

1 How many students voted? _____

2 How many students voted for white milk? _____

3 How many students voted for chocolate milk? _____

4 Draw two towers to show how the students voted.

Survey Questions and Secret Rules

Climb or Swim?

"Would you rather climb a mountain or swim in the ocean?"

Students answered this question by putting a cube under the picture of the mountain or under the picture of the ocean.

Family Connection

After taking a survey, students learned that they can make their own representations of the results. In Exercise 4, make sure that your child labels the data so that someone else looking at the information can tell what your child found out.

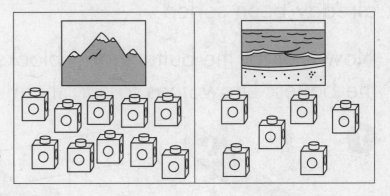

1 How many students wanted to climb a mountain? _____

2 How many students wanted to swim in the ocean? _____

3 How many students answered the survey? _____

4 Show this information in another way.

Mixed Review and Test Prep

5 How many flowers in all?

12	10	5	2
Ⓐ	Ⓑ	Ⓒ	Ⓓ

Which Box?

Look at the boxes. The buttons and blocks **inside** the boxes have already been sorted.

Family Connection

Today students were introduced to "Not-Boxes," which are open, flat boxes used to sort objects. All the items on one side have something in common. All the objects on the other side do not have that feature, or attribute, that unites the other objects. Ask your child to tell you the sorting rule for each exercise. Then suggest that he or she draw another item that would belong in each side of the box.

Now look at the buttons and blocks **below** the boxes. Draw lines to sort them!

1

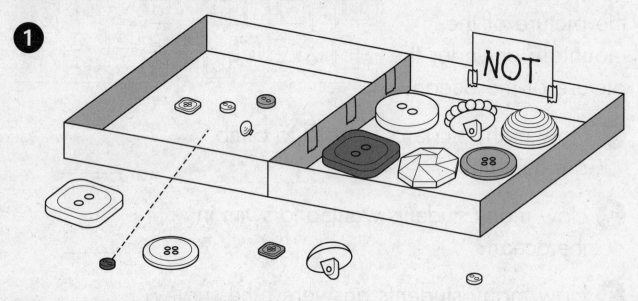

2

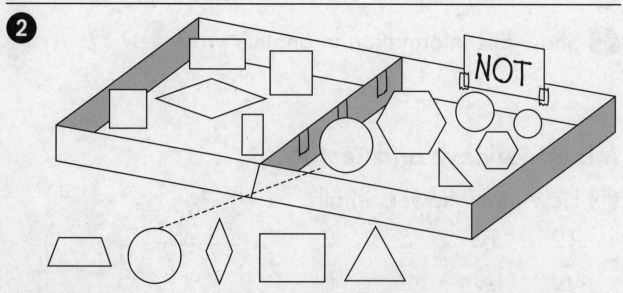

Use during Investigation 2 (Survey Questions), Sessions 3 and 4.

Name _____ Date _____

Taking a Survey

Some students were asked this question: "Would you rather be a dog or a tiger?" Their answers were recorded on this class list:

Family Connection

Pairs of students have been conducting surveys among their classmates to gather and record data. On this page, students are presented with a class list that shows **partial** results of a survey. Make sure your child notices that not all students have been surveyed since some names do not yet have a **T** or a **D** next to them.

Alec	T	Hailey	T	Kellin	D	Talia	D
Becky	D	Heidi		Kyle		Tomas	D
Blayke	D	Jack	D	Nick		Trevor	
Emma		Jessie		Olivia	T	Tyler	T
Evan	T	Jordan		Reese	T		

1 What do you think **T** stands for? _____

2 What do you think **D** stands for? _____

3 How many students were surveyed? _____

4 How many students were **not** surveyed? _____

Mixed Review and Test Prep

5 How many cubes should the next tower have?

3   4   6   9

Ⓐ   Ⓑ   Ⓒ   Ⓓ

© Pearson Education, Inc. 1

Name _____   Date _____

Looking at the Results

Survey question:
"Would you rather be
a dog or a tiger?"

> **Family Connection**
> In class, students completed a survey
> and came up with ways to show the
> results. Students might have used
> cubes, stick-on notes, pictures, numbers,
> or words. As your child makes a
> representation of the data based on
> the survey shown here, encourage him
> or her to show the results clearly
> and accurately.

Survey results:

Alec	T	Kellin	D
Becky	D	Kyle	T
Blayke	D	Nick	D
Emma	D	Olivia	T
Evan	T	Reese	T
Hailey	T	Talia	D
Heidi	D	Tomas	D
Jack	D	Trevor	T
Jessie	D	Tyler	T
Jordan	D		

1 Show the results in
a different way.

2 How many students would rather be a dog? _____

3 How many students would rather be a tiger? _____

4 Did more students want to be a dog or a tiger? _____

5 How many more? _____

76   *Use during Investigation 2 (Survey Questions), Sessions 5 and 6.*

© Pearson Education, Inc. 1

Name _____ Date _____

Presenting the Data

Family Connection

Students discussed and presented the results of their surveys. Have your child tell you about his or her survey. You may wish to have your child present the findings of the survey on this page, pretending that you are the audience. Suggest that your child study the representation so that he or she is familiar with it and can answer any questions you may have.

Would you rather live
in space or in a cave?

1 What was the question in this survey? _____

_____

2 How many students wanted to live in space? ____

3 How many students wanted to live in a cave? ____

4 How many students were surveyed? ____

Mixed Review and Test Prep

5 The goal is to collect 15 marbles.
How many more are needed?

 Ⓐ   Ⓑ   Ⓒ   Ⓓ

Room 110's Birthdays

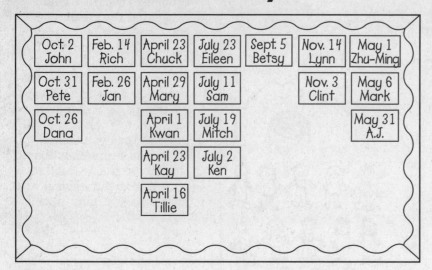

Oct. 2 John	Feb. 14 Rich	April 23 Chuck	July 23 Eileen	Sept. 5 Betsy	Nov. 14 Lynn	May 1 Zhu-Ming
Oct. 31 Pete	Feb. 26 Jan	April 29 Mary	July 11 Sam		Nov. 3 Clint	May 6 Mark
Oct. 26 Dana		April 1 Kwan	July 19 Mitch			May 31 A.J.
		April 23 Kay	July 2 Ken			
		April 16 Tillie				

Family Connection

Students have identified the date of each person's birth and then organized this information according to students' birth months. Students compared the data using terms such as **about the same, bigger than, smaller than, more,** and **less.** (At this time, the order of the months is not emphasized. The focus is on gathering and representing data.)

1 Which month has the most birthdays? _____

2 Which months have **no** birthdays? _____

_____

3 Which month has 4 birthdays? _____

4 Which months have the same number of birthdays?

_____

Mixed Review and Test Prep

5 How many cubes will be in the next step?

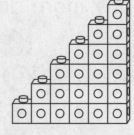

3   5   6   7

Ⓐ   Ⓑ   Ⓒ   Ⓓ

Special Day Lineup

1 Put this class's birthdays in order by writing **1** for the first date, **2** for the second date, and so on.

June 14	_____	**e**
March 2	_____	**s**
December 31	_____	**y**
October 30	_____	**a**
August 14	_____	**i**
September 19	_____	**l**
February 14	2	**y**
January 11	1	**m**
April 25	_____	**p**
September 1	_____	**a**
June 27	_____	**c**
September 23	_____	**d**

Family Connection

Students have been working with their partners, trying different ways to organize the class birth-date data. Then, as a class, students organized the data by months, in order, and by dates within the month. You may wish to have a calendar available for your child to use with this page. Have your child start with January and order the dates within a month as necessary. Help your child discover which months do not have any birthdays.

2 Find the letter next to each number, starting with 1. Write the letters on the lines below. What does the secret message say?

m	y	s	__	__	__	__	__	__	__	__	__
1	2	3	4	5	6	7	8	9	10	11	12

Survey Questions and Secret Rules

Month by Month ...

January	February	March
April	May	June
July	August	September
October	November	December

Family Connection

In class, students created a timeline to tell a story that takes place over one year. They drew pictures to tell the story of what happened during each month. On this page, students choose just 4 months, write the names of those months in order, and then draw or write about something that happens during each of those months. When your child is finished, ask him or her to tell you the story that the 4-month timeline shows.

Pick 4 months and circle their names.
Write the names of the months in order.
Draw or write about something that happens
in each month. (Use another sheet of paper
if you need to.)

1 _____

2 _____

3 _____

4 _____

Mixed Review and Test Prep

5 There are 5 birds eating.
5 more birds come to eat.
How many birds are eating now?

5	7	9	10
Ⓐ	Ⓑ	Ⓒ	Ⓓ

Name _____   Date _____

What Does It Show?

This chart shows how old some third grade students are.

Age	Number of Students
7	|
8	╫╫ ╫╫ ||
9	╫╫ ╫╫
10	

Family Connection

Today students collected data about their own ages and then used a variety of methods to represent, describe, and compare those data. To show that there are different ways of collecting and displaying the same information, tallies and cubes were used to represent the age of each student. Talk with your child about different ways he or she could show the information at left in a different way (on another sheet of paper). Perhaps he or she could draw pictures, use numbers or words, or use a combination of the three methods.

1 How many students are 7 years old? _____

2 How many students are 8 years old? _____

3 How many students are 9 years old? _____

4 How many students are 10 years old? _____

5 How old are most of the students? _____

6 Are there more 8-year-olds or

9-year-olds? _____

How many more? _____

7 Are there fewer 7-year-olds or

9-year-olds? _____

How many fewer? _____

Order in the Family!

Put the pictures in order from youngest to oldest.

Write **1, 2, 3, 4, 5,** and **6.**

1

 Grandpa Age 70    Mom Age 39    Dad Age 41    Taylor Age 5   Tyrone Age 3    Kraig Age 7

_____   _____   _____   _____   2   1

2

 Mom Age 28    Jenna Age 9    Auntie Sue Age 32    Wes Age 2    Janie Age 6    Gram Age 53

_____   _____   _____   _____   _____   _____

I can find the numbers on the 100 chart!

1	2	3	4	5	6	7	8	9	10
11	12	13	14	15	16	17	18	19	20
21	22	23	24	25	26	27	28	29	30
31	32	33	34	35	36	37	38	39	40
41	42	43	44	45	46	47	48	49	50
51	52	53	54	55	56	57	58	59	60
61	62	63	64	65	66	67	68	69	70
71	72	73	74	75	76	77	78	79	80
81	82	83	84	85	86	87	88	89	90
91	92	93	94	95	96	97	98	99	100

Mystery People

Solve the riddle.
Then write the mystery
person's name.

Mary  Age 3

Maddie  Age 8

Forrest  Age 12

Dad  Age 35

Mom  Age 37

Papa  Age 67

1 I am older than Forrest. I am younger than Papa.
I am older than 36. Who am I? _____

2 I am younger than Mom. I am older than 3.
I am younger than 12. Who am I? _____

3 I am older than 12. I am older than Dad.
I am older than 40. Who am I? _____

4 I am younger than 52. I am older than Maddie.
I am younger than Dad. Who am I? _____

Mixed Review and Test Prep

5 How many rectangles are in this pattern?

□ □ □ □ □ □ □ □ □

13   12   9   6
Ⓐ   Ⓑ   Ⓒ   Ⓓ

How Many?

The chart shows how many students are in class today and how many are not.

Room 110's Attendance	
HERE	**NOT HERE**
☆☆☆ ☆☆☆ ☆☆☆ ☆☆☆ ☆☆☆	☆ ☆ ☆ ☆ ☆ ☆

❶ How many students are here today? _____

❷ How many students are absent today? _____

❸ How many students are in the class? _____

Mixed Review and Test Prep

❹ How many hands and feet in all?

   10   20   22   40
   Ⓐ   Ⓑ   Ⓒ   Ⓓ

Survey Questions and Secret Rules

Room 110's Unusual Day

Here are 2 attendance charts.

White stars tell how many present.
Gray stars tell how many absent.

Family Connection
Students compared attendance data from a "usual" day of school (more students present than absent) with data from an "unusual" day (more students absent than present). Students also created representations of the imaginary unusual day. You may wish to ask your child to make one or more representations of the data presented on this page. Remind your child to keep track of the number of children in each of the four groups.

A Usual Day		An Unusual Day	
HERE	**NOT HERE**	**HERE**	**NOT HERE**

Chart A   **Chart B**

1 On the **usual** day, _____ students were in school, and only

_____ students were absent.

2 On the **unusual** day, _____ students were in school, and

_____ students were absent!

Name _____ Date _____

Quilt Squares and Block Towns

Same Shape?

Look at the first shape in the row. Circle the objects that are the same shape.

Family Connection

Today students were presented with a variety of 2- and 3-dimensional shapes and asked to think about familiar objects that have these shapes. Read the name of each shape with your child and ask your child what he or she notices about it. Then invite your child to go on a "Shape Hunt," looking for objects in your home or neighborhood that have these same (or similar) shapes.

1  Cylinder

2  Rectangular Prism

3 Sphere

4 Cone

Mixed Review and Test Prep

5 How many flowers are in the vase?

12   11   10   9

Ⓐ   Ⓑ   Ⓒ   Ⓓ

© Pearson Education, Inc. **1**

How Many in All?

Write how many of each shape. Then write how many blocks in all.

1 Shape 1

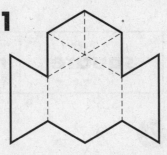

Shape	⬡	⬟	▱	▢	◇	△
How many?	_____	_____	_____	_____	_____	_____

Total blocks _____

2 Shape 2

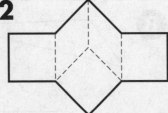

Shape	⬡	⬟	▱	▢	◇	△
How many?	_____	_____	_____	_____	_____	_____

Total blocks _____

Quilt Squares and Block Towns

You Name It!

Write the name of
each shape.

Family Connection

In the "Quick Images with Shapes" activity, a shape
is shown to students for about 5 seconds; then the
image is hidden and students try to draw what they
saw. Then the same shape is shown again and
students tell what they noticed about the shape and
how they knew that it was, for example, a square
and not a triangle.

triangle	circle	square	rectangle

1 _____

2 _____

3 _____

4 _____

5 _____

6 _____

7 _____

8 _____

9 Draw a shape with 4 sides.

How Many Blocks?

Look at the flower pattern.
Write how many of each kind
of block are used in it.

1 How many hexagons?

_____

2 How many trapezoids?

_____

3 How many triangles?

_____

4 How many squares?

_____

5 How many rhombuses like this?

_____

6 How many rhombuses like this?

_____

7 How many blocks in all?

_____

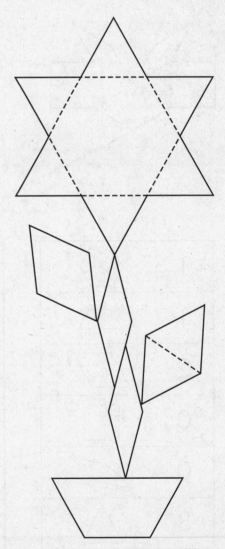

Quilt Squares and Block Towns

The Match Game

Family Connection

Previously, students were given designs and filled them in with pattern blocks. Today, students were given a total number of pattern blocks, and had to make designs using that number of blocks. The designs were then recorded by tracing around the blocks. Then the number of each kind of block was recorded.

1 Write how many blocks were used in each design.

2 Then match each design with the chart that tells how many of each kind were used.

Design 1 _____   **Design 2** _____   **Design 3** _____

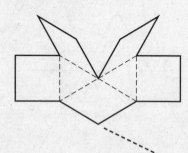   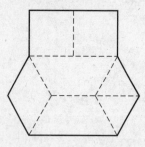   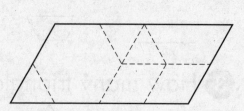

Design 1		Design 2		Design 3	
1	⬡	0	⬡	0	⬡
1	⏢	0	⏢	2	⏢
2	▱	1	▱	1	▱
0	▢	2	▢	2	▢
0	◇	2	◇	0	◇
3	△	2	△	2	△

Name _____ Date _____

And the Total Is ...

1 Color pattern blocks to make a design. Then fill in the chart to tell how many of each kind of block you used in your design.

Family Connection

In class, students were given information about how many blocks were used to make a design and then had to figure out how many blocks were used altogether. Here, your child is challenged to create his or her own design and then analyze it.

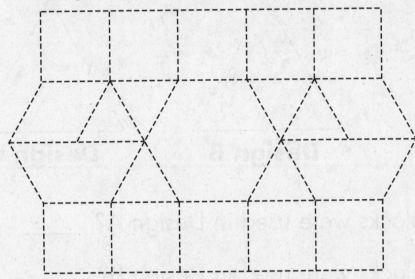

Shape	⬡	⬭	▱	☐	△	Total
How many?						

Mixed Review and Test Prep

2 This train should have 12 cubes. How many more cubes are needed?

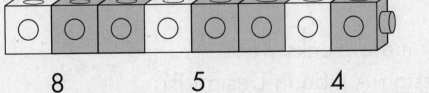

8   5   4   3
Ⓐ   Ⓑ   Ⓒ   Ⓓ

Three Designs

Look at the designs.
Answer the questions.

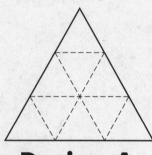
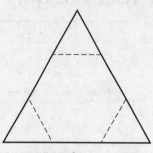
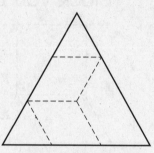

Design A   **Design B**   **Design C**

1 How many blocks were used in Design A? _____

2 How many blocks were used in Design B? _____

3 How many blocks were used in Design C? _____

4 Which design used the **fewest** blocks? _____

5 Which design used the **most** blocks? _____

6 How many triangles were used in Design C? _____

7 Which design used the most triangles? _____

8 How many more blocks were
used in Design A than in Design B? _____

Name _____ Date _____

Quilt Squares and Block Towns

What Do You See?

Draw a line to match the sentence with a shape or shapes.

Family Connection

The class has been working on a more complex version of the "Quick Images with Shapes" activity in which the teacher shows a single shape image or a combination of shapes, and students quickly draw what they see. **Questions you might ask your child:** "What shapes make up the combination shapes?" "How many sides does each shape have?"

1 I see a triangle.

2 I see a square inside a circle.

3 I see a trapezoid on top of a rectangle.

4 I see a circle inside a square.

5 I see a shape with no straight lines.

Mixed Review and Test Prep

6 Which number is greater than ⬜ 8 ?

6	7	8	9
Ⓐ	Ⓑ	Ⓒ	Ⓓ

Which Design Am I?

Which design solves the riddle?
Write **A, B,** or **C.**

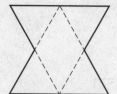 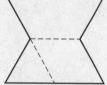 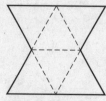

Design A   **Design B**   **Design C**

> **Family Connection**
>
> Students have been filling outlines of designs in different ways, and in the process learning how shapes can be combined or taken apart to make other shapes. Students are becoming increasingly familiar with equivalencies among shapes in the pattern block set. Ask your child to show you some of these equivalencies in the designs on this page. For example, when comparing Designs B and C, your child can see that 3 triangles fill a trapezoid and 2 triangles fill a rhombus.

1 I have a rhombus.
I have the least number of blocks.
Which design am I? _____

2 I have more than 3 blocks.
I have only one kind of block.
Which design am I? _____

3 I have a rhombus.
I have only two kinds of blocks.
Which design am I? _____

4 I have more than one triangle.
I have the most blocks.
Which design am I? _____

5 I have fewer than 6 blocks.
I have 3 different kinds of blocks.
Which design am I? _____

Quilt Squares and Block Towns

Fill Them Up!

Circle the shapes
that fill the shape
on the left.

Family Connection
As students continue to fill outlines of designs with pattern blocks, they are developing their ability to see equivalencies among the shapes. This helps students determine ways to fill the outline of a design using the greatest or least number of blocks.

1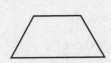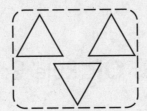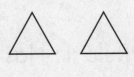

2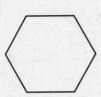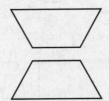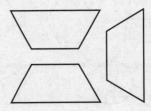

3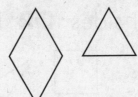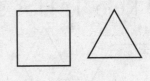

4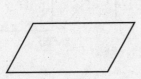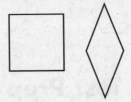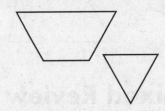

Mixed Review and Test Prep

5 How many more chairs are needed?

   12   10   3   2
   Ⓐ   Ⓑ   Ⓒ   Ⓓ

People	Chairs
12	10

Quilt Squares and Block Towns

Follow the Rules

Choose a rule and circle it.
Then circle the shapes that fit
the rule.

Family Connection
Students' work has been focusing
on describing, comparing, sorting,
and classifying 2-dimensional
shapes. Here your child chooses
a way to sort a set of shapes,
and then circles the shapes that
fit the sorting rule. Ask your child
to tell you the names of any of
the shapes that he or she knows.

1 Rule 1: Has 4 sides **OR** Rule 2: Has curves

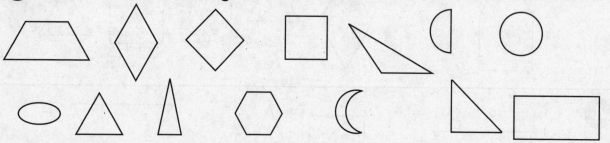

2 Rule 1: Has straight sides **OR** Rule 2: Has 3 corners

Mixed Review and Test Prep

3 Mark had 8 baseball cards. He gave
3 to his friend Ben. How many baseball
cards does Mark have now?

11	8	7	5
Ⓐ	Ⓑ	Ⓒ	Ⓓ

Take a Closer Look

1 Draw a line under
each triangle.

2 How many sides do triangles have? _____

3 How many corners? _____

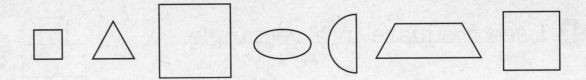

4 Draw a line under each square.

5 How many sides do squares have? _____

6 How many corners? _____

Mixed Review and Test Prep

7 Jill's pen is 7 cubes long. Maria's pen is shorter.
How many cubes long is Maria's pen?

11	9	8	6
Ⓐ	Ⓑ	Ⓒ	Ⓓ

What Do You See?

Match the sentence
to the shapes.

Family Connection
Today students were shown a single shape or
combination of shapes for about 5 seconds; then the
image was hidden and students tried to draw what
they saw. On this page, students read or listen to
a description of a shape or combination of shapes,
and then match the description to the drawing.

1 I see a circle in a triangle.

2 I see a rectangle under
a square.

3 I see a triangle on top of
a circle.

4 I see a square in a rectangle.

5 I see 2 circles in a rectangle.

6 I see a rhombus next to
a square.

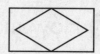

7 I see a square in a circle.

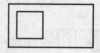

8 I see a rhombus in
a rectangle.

Quilt Squares and Block Towns

Quilt Patterns

Look at Patterns A and B. Answer the questions.

Pattern A

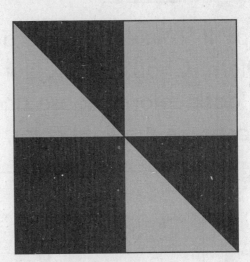

Pattern B

1 How many black triangles are in Pattern A? _____

2 How many gray triangles are in Pattern A? _____

3 How many white triangles are in Pattern A? _____

4 How many black triangles are in Pattern B? _____

5 How many gray triangles are in Pattern B? _____

6 How many black squares are in Pattern B? _____

7 How many gray squares are in Pattern B? _____

Make Your Own Quilt!

Look at this quilt square.

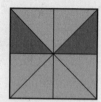

Copy it 9 times to make a quilt pattern. Choose one color to be the dark color. Choose another color to be the light color.

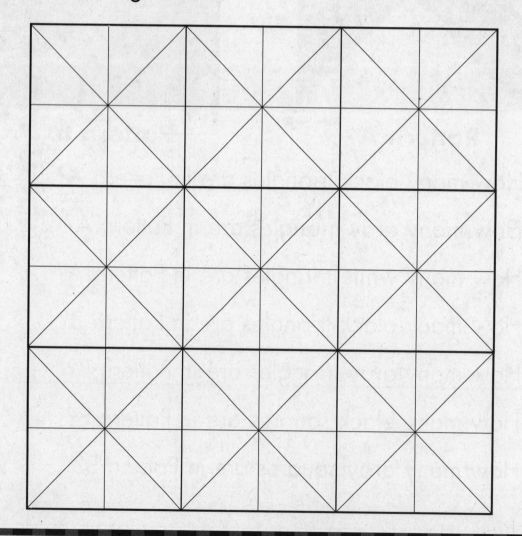

Use after Investigation 1 (2-D Shapes and Patterns), Sessions 13, 14, and 15.

© Pearson Education, Inc. **1**

Quilt Squares and Block Towns

Cube Things

Look at these
Cube Things.

Family Connection
Students used interlocking cubes to copy a given "Cube Thing." (A "Cube Thing" is made of 8–12 interlocking cubes.) Students then used additional cubes to construct an exact match of the original "Thing." (Note that the colors do not need to match when a copy is being constructed.)

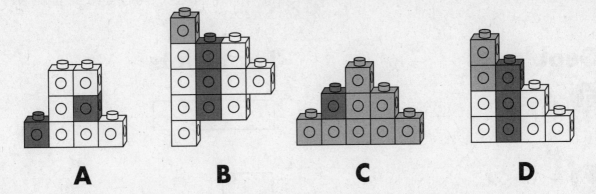

A　　　　**B**　　　　**C**　　　　**D**

1 Write the letter of the Cube Thing above
that matches the Cube Thing below.
(REMEMBER: The colors do not need to match.)

  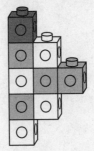 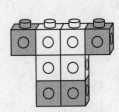

_____　　_____　　_____　　_____

2 How many cubes are in Thing A? _____

3 How many cubes are in Thing B? _____

4 How many cubes are in Thing C? _____

5 How many cubes are in Thing D? _____

Name _____   Date _____

Make the Match

Match each Geoblock to a footprint.

Geoblocks

1

2

3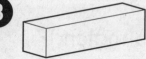

4

5

Footprints

6 What is the name of Geoblock 1's footprint? _____

7 What is the name of Geoblock 2's footprint? _____

8 What is the name of Geoblock 3's footprint? _____

Is It a Match?

Does the picture match the sentence? If it **does,** circle the picture. If it **doesn't,** cross out the picture.

1 I have a side shaped like a **triangle.**

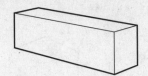 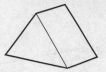

2 I have a side shaped like a **rectangle.**

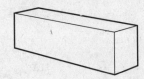 

3 I have a side shaped like a **square.**

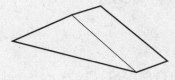 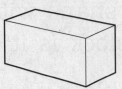

Mixed Review and Test Prep

4 Which group below shows more beans than this group?

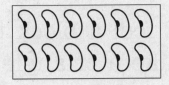

 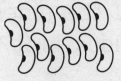

Name _____   Date _____

What Is Inside That Sock?

Look at the Geoblocks.
Imagine that you are
reaching into a sock
that has these
4 blocks inside.

Family Connection

Students have been participating in an activity called "Blocks in a Sock". They were shown pictures of 2 or 3 Geoblocks and told that these blocks had been put into a sock. Students took turns reaching into the sock and trying to pick out a specific block just by feeling it. You may wish to ask your child to describe how the Geoblocks in the pictures are the same and how they are different.

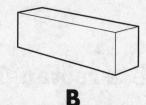

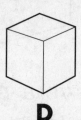

A   B   C   D

1 I feel a shape like a box.
Which block is it?   _____

2 I feel a shape with a pointy top.
Which block is it?   _____

3 I feel a block that has a long and
skinny side. Which block is it?   _____

4 I feel a block that has a side shaped
like a triangle. Which block is it?   _____

5 I feel a block and all of the sides
feel the same. Which block is it?   _____

Use during Investigation 2 (Comparing and Constructing 3-D Shapes), Sessions 4, 5, and 6.

Quilt Squares and Block Towns

Let's Make a Copy

Look at the shape. Make the same shape on the grid.

1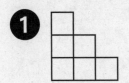

2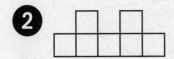

3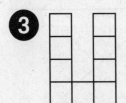

4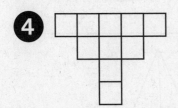

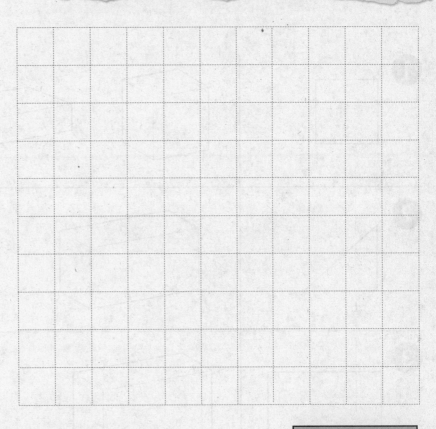

Mixed Review and Test Prep

5 There are 23 children in the class. Three children are **not** here today. How many children **are** here today?

Not Here Today
Kim
Brighid
Rocco

26
(A)

23
(B)

21
(C)

20
(D)

Use during Investigation 2 (Comparing and Constructing 3-D Shapes), Sessions 4, 5, and 6.

Quilt Squares and Block Towns

More Footprints

Look at the footprint. Then circle the Geoblock that makes that footprint.

Family Connection

Students are learning to find blocks that have faces (or sides) that match given outlines. Have your child tell you how he or she decides which block has a face that matches a given "footprint." Encourage your child to use the words **square, triangle,** and **rectangle** to describe both 2-dimensional footprints and certain faces of 3-dimensional shapes. As students build their mathematics vocabulary over time, they will deepen their understanding of each shape (and learn that a square is a "special kind of rectangle").

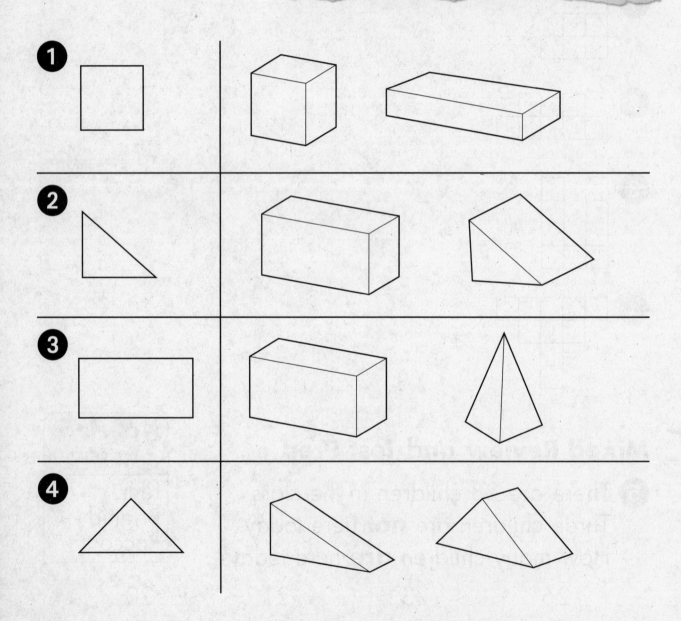

Quilt Squares and Block Towns

Size and Shape

Look at the boxes.

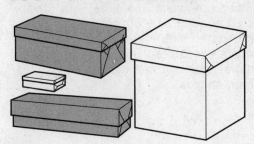

Family Connection
Students have been looking at "Mystery Boxes," variously sized and empty boxes that were covered in paper so that what they originally contained was unknown. After considering the size and shape of each box, students visualized what it might have contained. Students also discovered that every box has 6 flat sides, or faces.

1 How are they different? _____

_____

_____

Find the two things that will **best** fit into each box.
Write the letters under the box.

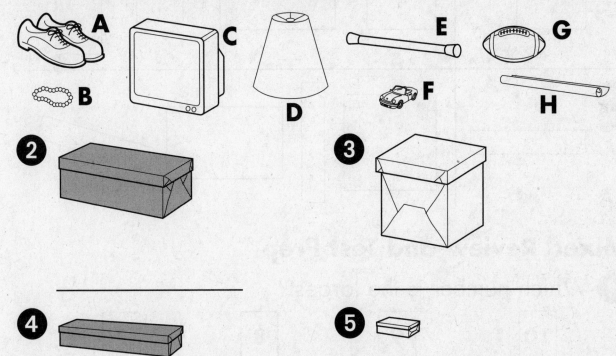

Same or Different?

Look at the first shape in the row. Then draw a line under the shapes that are the same size and shape.

Family Connection

Students constructed their own boxes out of cardboard rectangles and then compared the sizes and shapes of the boxes. Students learned several characteristics of a rectangular prism, including how faces come together at edges, and how opposite sides are the same size and shape. Building a box out of flat pieces helps students develop an understanding of how 2-dimensional shapes can be put together to make 3-dimensional shapes.

Mixed Review and Test Prep

4 Which number is the largest?

10	9	8	7
Ⓐ	Ⓑ	Ⓒ	Ⓓ

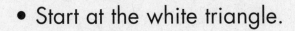

Quilt Squares and Block Towns

Make the Mystery Shape

1 Draw lines to connect the 6 shapes.

- Start at the white triangle.

- Go to the gray rhombus.

- Go to the white trapezoid.

- Go to the black square.

- Go to the gray triangle.

- Go to the black trapezoid.

- Go back to the white triangle.

2 The mystery shape is a _____.

3 How many sides does it have? _____

Mixed Review and Test Prep

4 There are 9 counters in all. How many are under the cup?

4	5	6	9
Ⓐ	Ⓑ	Ⓒ	Ⓓ

Name _____   Date _____

Cube Boxes

Match each box with the object that would fit **best** inside the box.

Family Connection

Students have been making boxes using cardboard rectangles. To extend the activity, interlocking cubes were used to make a box that could hold a small object. Help your child consider which object would fit best in each interlocking-cube box on this page.

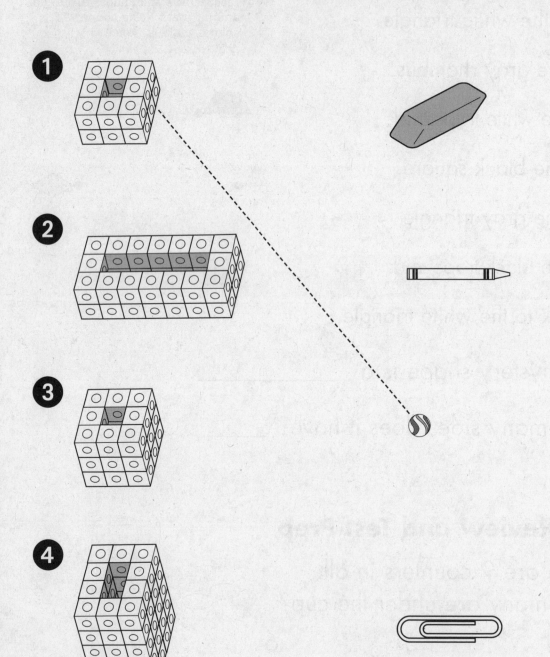

①

②

③

④

Quilt Squares and Block Towns

Draw a 3-D Object!

1 Find a box.
Look at it very carefully.
Then draw a picture of it.

Family Connection

Students have been building structures with Geoblocks and then drawing what they have made. Students are developing an understanding of the difference between 2-dimensional (2-D) and 3-dimensional (3-D) space, and how a picture that is two-dimensional (flat) on a piece of paper can look three-dimensional. Many students' first drawing attempts look 2-dimensional. Encourage your child to look at the faces of the box and how they come together.

Mixed Review and Test Prep

2 There are some beads in the counting jar. There are more than 10 beads. How many beads could be in the jar?

Counting Jar

13   10   9   5

Ⓐ   Ⓑ   Ⓒ   Ⓓ

Building with Boxes

1 Find several boxes.
Make a building.
Then draw a picture of it.

Family Connection

Students continue drawing in
three dimensions. Help your child
focus on observing, describing,
and comparing the 3-D shapes
that he or she is drawing. Point
to a shape in the picture and
ask your child to tell you what
part of the building that shape
represents. Ask, "How [from
what perspective] were you
looking at your building as you
drew this part?" Remember to
focus on careful observation and
description, rather than on
drawing skill.

Mixed Review and Test Prep

2 How many tails?

2   5   6   8
Ⓐ   Ⓑ   Ⓒ   Ⓓ

3 How many eyes?

16   13   12   6
Ⓐ   Ⓑ   Ⓒ   Ⓓ

Quilt Squares and Block Towns

List Some Buildings

1 Write the names of some buildings that you have seen or know about. Try to think of buildings with different kinds of shapes.

_____

_____

_____

_____

_____

_____

_____

Mixed Review and Test Prep

2 Which object is shaped like this?

Quilt Squares and Block Towns

Picture This!

1 Draw a picture of a building you have seen.

Family Connection

Pairs of students have been drawing plans for a building that will be part of a 3-dimensional town the class will be creating in the next math session. Each pair of students used no more than 12 blocks, and their building had to fit on a 5-by-8-inch sheet of paper. Observe your child as he or she draws a building in which different shapes are visible.

Mixed Review and Test Prep

2 Which cards are in order from **least** to **greatest**?

3 5 4	7 5 3	6 8 10	2 4 1
Ⓐ	Ⓑ	Ⓒ	Ⓓ

3 Which date is missing on the calendar?

18   19   20   21
Ⓐ   Ⓑ   Ⓒ   Ⓓ

September						
Sunday	Monday	Tuesday	Wednesday	Thursday	Friday	Saturday
	1	2	3	4	5	6
7	8	9	10	11	12	13
14	15	16	17	18	19	
21	22	23	24	25	26	27
28	29	30				

Quilt Squares and Block Towns

Shape Town

Look at the town
made of Geoblocks.
Write what you see.

Family Connection
Students used Geoblocks to make buildings and then
wrote several sentences describing them. As your child
describes the buildings in this drawing, ask questions
that help him or her compare the buildings: "Which
buildings have rectangular faces?" "Do any buildings
look like a cube?" "Which buildings have similar shapes?"

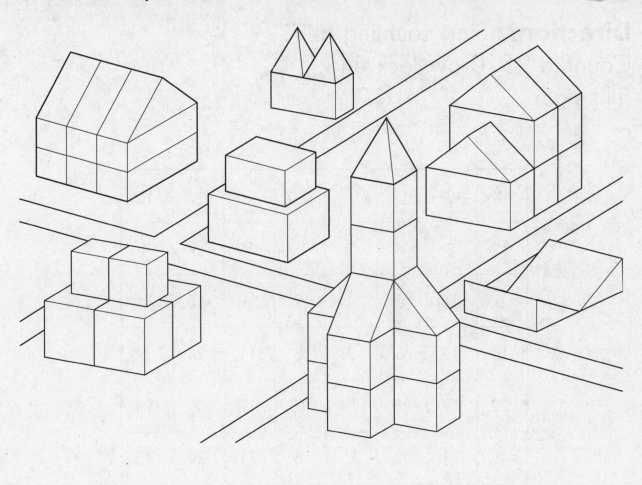

_____

_____

_____

_____

_____

Can You Follow Directions?

Jack and Jill are going to play baseball. Help them follow the directions to get to the field.

Directions: Start counting at 1. Count to 25. Draw Jack and Jill's path.

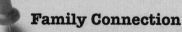

Family Connection

Students have been giving directions for getting from one place to another in the classroom, using paces and turns. This activity introduces them to the idea of "motion through space." Students estimate distance, choose directions, and decide how to turn in order to change directions.

1----2	11	6	20	8	17	12
12	3	4	2	19	23	5	1
5	15	5	1	9	10	18	15
10	12	6	7	8	11	24	6
22	3	19	14	13	12	2	14
7	21	16	15	6	21	22	23
16	13	17	18	19	20	9	24
9	4	7	5	11	8	10	25

Quilt Squares and Block Towns

Where Are You?

Use the map to
answer the questions.

Family Connection
Students used a map of the class town they created
in Session 5 to create paths showing how they could
get from one location to another. Using a small block
or counter to represent a person, students then
provided directions telling the "person" how many
city blocks to walk straight ahead, and when and in
which direction to turn, if necessary.

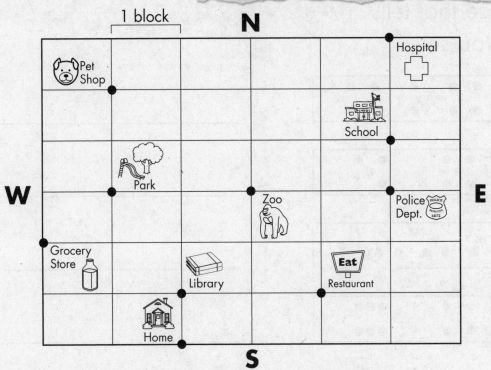

1 block   N

Pet Shop   Hospital   School   Zoo   Police Dept.   Park   Grocery Store   Library   Eat Restaurant   Home

W   E

S

1 Start at the Pet Shop. Go 4 blocks east.
Go 1 block south. Where are you? _____

2 Start at the Library. Go 2 blocks north.
Go 1 block west. Where are you? _____

3 Start at the Hospital. Go 3 blocks south.
Go 5 blocks west. Go 1 block south.
Where are you? _____

4 Start at the School. Go 3 blocks west.
Go 4 blocks south. Where are you? _____

Number Games and Story Problems

What Does 10 Look Like?

Look at each group of dots. Write a number sentence that tells what you see.

 1

$$4 + 2 + 4 = 10$$

2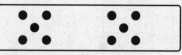

_____

3

_____

4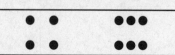

_____

Mixed Review and Test Prep

5 How many triangles would fill the hexagon?

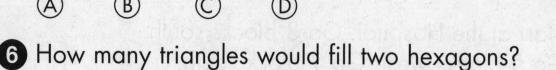

  2   4   5   6
 (A)   (B)   (C)   (D)

6 How many triangles would fill two hexagons?

 14   12   5   6
 (A)   (B)   (C)   (D)

Dot-Card Combinations

1 Make 12 in all by drawing dots on the blank card.

  [blank card]

Family Connection
Students have been finding combinations of given numbers using dot addition cards. They then record the combinations. For example, students may write 4 + 5 as a combination for 9. You may wish to ask your child to record the addition combination for each exercise on another sheet of paper.

2 Make 10 in all by drawing dots on the blank card.

    [blank card]

3 Make 15 in all by drawing dots on the blank card.

    [blank card]

4 Make 12 in all by drawing dots on the blank card.

   [blank card]

5 Make 10 in all by drawing dots on the blank card.

  [blank card]

Number Games and Story Problems

12 in All

There are 12 counters in all.
Write how many are **on** the paper.
Write how many are **off** the paper.

Family Connection

Students have been playing **On and Off,** a game in which they toss a given number of counters over a sheet of paper and then record how many of them land on and off the paper. This activity generates different combinations for the given number.

 1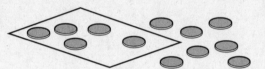

On the paper _____

Off the paper _____

 2

On the paper _____

Off the paper _____

 3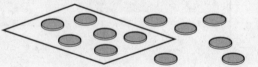

On the paper _____

Off the paper _____

 4

On the paper _____

Off the paper _____

 5

On the paper _____

Off the paper _____

 6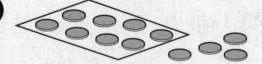

On the paper _____

Off the paper _____

Number Games and Story Problems

Give Me 10!

Write a number on the card to make 10 in all.

Family Connection

Today students learned a new game in which they make combinations of 10 using number cards, and then record the combinations using number expressions such as 3 + 7 and 4 + 1 + 5. You may wish to ask your child to record the combinations of 10 that he or she makes on this page.

1 | 2 | 8 |

2 | 5 |

3 | 2 | 4 | |

4 | 7 |

5 | 1 | 8 | |

6 | 10 | |

7 | 2 | 2 | |

8 | 3 | 6 | |

9 | 1 | |

10 | 5 | 3 | |

Number Games and Story Problems

Which Combination?

The dot cards show 12.
Circle the combination that
matches the cards.

Family Connection

Students have been recording combinations of numbers they find while playing **Dot Addition,** a game in which they make a given number by adding the dots found in a set of dot cards. Each set of cards on this page shows a different combination of 12.

1

2 + 4 + 5

2 + 5 + 5

2

4 + 3 + 5

4 + 5 + 2

3

1 + 5 + 6

6 + 2 + 5

4

7 + 4

4 + 8

Mixed Review and Test Prep

5 Which tower has the most cubes?

Ⓐ A

Ⓑ B

Ⓒ C

Ⓓ D

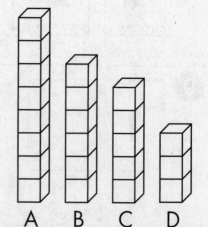

A   B   C   D

Name _____   Date _____

10 Shapes in All

Draw **squares, triangles,** or **circles** so that each box has 10 shapes in all. Then record what you did.

Family Connection
Today students solved problems in which they had to find combinations of two or more different-colored crayons so that there were 10 crayons in all, and then recorded the combinations on paper. This activity requires students to combine quantities, combine numbers, and record solutions.

1

I drew ___2 triangles___ .

2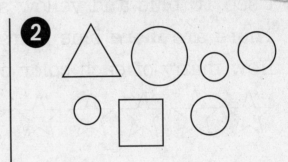

I drew _____ .

3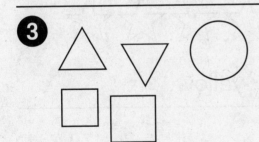

I drew _____ .

4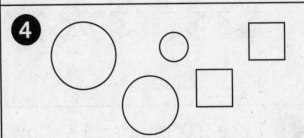

I drew _____ .

Star Riddles

Solve each riddle.
Color the stars to help you.

Family Connection
Today students solved Crayon Puzzles: they were given a total number of red and blue crayons and then a clue about how many of each color there were. On this page your child is given a total number of stars and then has to determine how many of each color there are, or could be, based on the clue that is provided.

1 I see 10 blue and yellow stars.
There are **more** blue stars.
How many of each color could there be?

_____ blue   _____ yellow

2 I see 10 blue and yellow stars.
There is the **same number** of each color.
How many of each color are there?

_____ blue   _____ yellow

3 I see 10 blue and yellow stars.
There are **fewer** blue stars.
How many of each color could there be?

_____ blue   _____ yellow

Number Games and Story Problems

Inside and Outside

There are **9** soccer balls in all. Write how many are **outside** the bag. Write how many are **inside** the bag.

Family Connection

Students have been playing a game called **Counters in a Cup:** They are told how many counters there are in all, and then they have to determine how many counters are hiding under a cup after counting how many are outside the cup.

1

Outside _____

Inside _____

2

Outside _____

Inside _____

3

Outside _____

Inside _____

4

Outside _____

Inside _____

Mixed Review and Test Prep

5 Which group of marbles matches the number of cubes?

Ⓐ   Ⓑ   Ⓒ   Ⓓ

Name _____ Date _____

Jack and Jill

Where are Jack and Jill going?

Family Connection

Students continue to find combinations of 10 and then share what they find with classmates. To help your child follow Jack and Jill's path, provide him or her with counters for use in modeling each combination, as necessary. It may help to have your child cross out each combination that does not equal 10.

1 Draw a line connecting the combinations of 10 to find out.

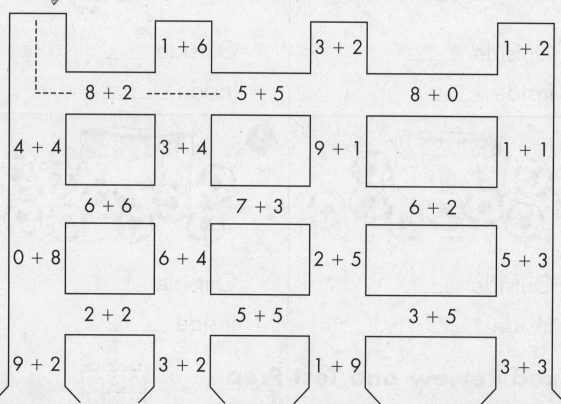

1 + 6   3 + 2   1 + 2

8 + 2   5 + 5   8 + 0

4 + 4   3 + 4   9 + 1   1 + 1

6 + 6   7 + 3   6 + 2

0 + 8   6 + 4   2 + 5   5 + 3

2 + 2   5 + 5   3 + 5

9 + 2   3 + 2   1 + 9   3 + 3

House

Zoo

Beach

Amusement Park

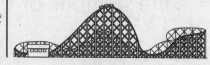

2 Circle the place where Jack and Jill are going.

Name _____ Date _____

Tell Me a Story

Match the number story with the number sentence.

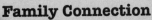

Family Connection
Today students listened to a number story that shows different combinations of a number; then they created their own number-combination stories. Here your child is shown pictures that represent different combinations of 9 and 12. Have him or her tell a story that goes with each picture and its matching equation.

1 12 children are playing.

$4 + 4 + 1 = 9$

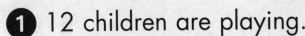

2 12 children are playing.

$3 + 6 = 9$

3 9 children are playing.

$5 + 7 = 12$

4 9 children are playing.

$6 + 3 + 3 = 12$

Name _____   Date _____

Number Games and Story Problems

Pairs of Things

Write how many
are in each group.

> **Family Connection**
> Students have been working on finding the total of
> things that come in pairs, thereby developing meaning
> for counting by 2's. At this time the focus is on how
> a solution is found, not just on finding a total. Tell
> your child that he or she can use counters, fingers,
> pictures, or anything else to solve each problem.

1    _8_

2       _____

3     _____

4        _____

5      _____

Mixed Review and Test Prep

6 Which shape has 4 sides?

Ⓐ   Ⓑ   Ⓒ   Ⓓ

128 *Use after Investigation 2 (Twos, Fives, and Tens), Session 1.*

© Pearson Education, Inc. 1

Number Games and Story Problems

Counting Feet

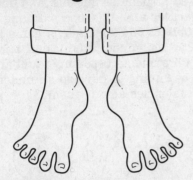

Complete the chart.
Write how many feet there are.

	People	Feet
1	1	2
2	2	
3	3	
4	4	
5	5	
6	6	
7	7	
8	8	
9	9	
10	10	

Name _____   Date _____

Number Games and Story Problems

Collecting Coins

1 Circle coins to show **15¢** in all.

Family Connection

Today students looked at pennies, nickels, and dimes and discussed similarities and differences among them. They played **Collect 25¢ Together,** a game in which they collect 25¢ using pennies, nickels, and/or dimes. The focus is on students becoming familiar with the coins, and beginning to develop an understanding of the equivalencies among them.

2 Circle coins to show **20¢** in all.

3 Circle coins to show **25¢** in all.

130   *Use after Investigation 2 (Twos, Fives, and Tens), Session 3.*

© Pearson Education, Inc. **1**

Name _____   Date _____

Number Games and Story Problems

Counting Squares

Write how many
squares are in
each group.

Family Connection
Students have been finding how many squares are
in a given group, an activity that encourages them to
develop strategies for organizing the sets of squares
so that they are easy to combine and count. On this
page, the squares are already arranged in ways that
suggest a way to count them (such as by counting all
the pairs and then the single squares).

1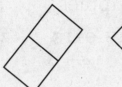

_____

2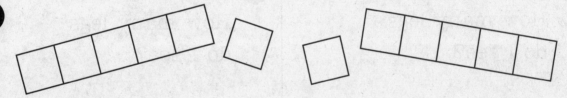

_____

3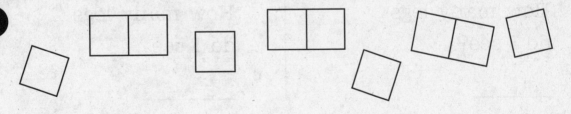

_____

4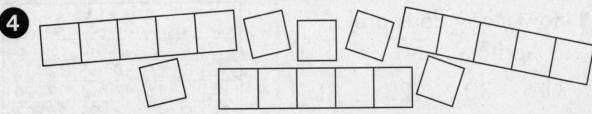

_____

© Pearson Education, Inc. 1

*Use during Investigation 2 (Twos, Fives, and Tens), Sessions 4 and 5.* **131**

Number Games and Story Problems

How Many Do I See?

Solve each riddle.

Family Connection

Students have been solving problems in which they find the total of several equal amounts and then record how they solved the problem, using pictures, words, and/or numbers. Ask your child to tell you how he or she thinks about and solves one or more of the riddles on this page. (You may need to remind your child that spiders have 8 legs, and ants have 6.)

1 I see 4 boys.
How many eyes
do I see?

_____

2 I see 5 puppies.
How many ears
do I see?

_____

3 I see 3 horses.
How many legs
do I see?

_____

4 I see 2 spiders.
How many legs
do I see?

_____

5 I see 6 birds.
How many legs
do I see?

_____

6 I see 6 ants.
How many legs
do I see?

_____

Mixed Review and Test Prep

7 How many days are
in April?

	April					
Sunday	Monday	Tuesday	Wednesday	Thursday	Friday	Saturday
	1	2	3	4	5	6
7	8	9	10	11	12	13
14	15	16	17	18	19	20
21	22	23	24	25	26	27
28	29	30				

31   30   23   1
Ⓐ   Ⓑ   Ⓒ   Ⓓ

Name _____   Date _____

Number Games and Story Problems

Counting to 100

Fill in the missing numbers.
Look for patterns. Tell someone
at home about the patterns
you find.

Family Connection

Today students played **Missing Numbers,** a game in which they identify numbers that are missing from a 100 chart. After your child completes this 100 chart, talk about patterns that he or she sees: "What is the same in the first and second columns?" "What changes in each row?"

1	2	3	4	5		7	8	9	10
11		13	14	15	16		18	19	20
21	22	23			26	27	28		30
31	32	33	34	35		37	38	39	
41		43	44	45	46	47	48	49	50
	52	53	54	55	56		58		60
61			64		66	67	68	69	
71	72	73		75		77		79	80
	82		84	85	86	87		89	90
91			94		96		98	99	

© Pearson Education, Inc. 1

Name _____   Date _____

Number Games and Story Problems

Collecting MORE Coins!

Circle coins to show how much each child collected.

> **Family Connection**
>
> Students have been playing **Collect 25¢ Together,** the game in which they collect coins that total 25¢ (or a bit more). Your child may choose to count money amounts using only pennies or using a combination of coins. The focus is on students becoming familiar with the coins, and with the equivalencies among them. (If possible, give your child real coins to work with; then talk with each other about the various ways a given amount can be represented.)

1 Juan collected **9¢.**

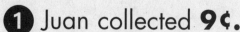

2 Matt collected **15¢.**

3 Becky collected **25¢.**

Mixed Review and Test Prep

4 There are 9 counters in all. How many counters are under the cup?

   2   3   4   5

   Ⓐ   Ⓑ   Ⓒ   Ⓓ

Counting MORE Squares!

Write how many squares are in each group.

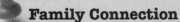

1

_____

2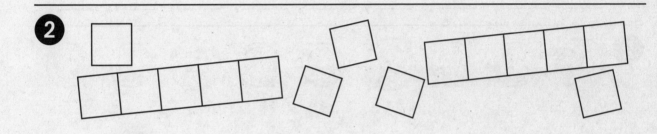

_____

3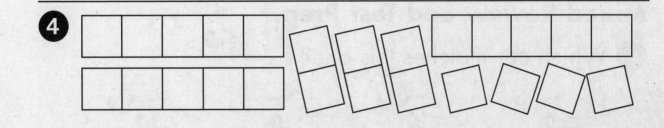

_____

4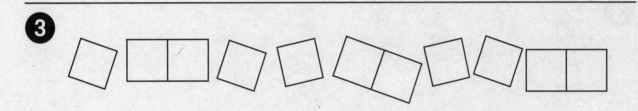

_____

Name _____   Date _____

Number Games and Story Problems

Show Me
the Pattern!

Show the pattern
another way. You can
use colors, shapes,
drawings, or numbers.

Family Connection

Students are learning that a repeating pattern can
be represented in different ways: using physical
actions, concrete materials, drawings, or numbers.
For example, a simple slap knees-slap knees-clap-clap-
clap sound and movement pattern can be represented
using shapes (circle-circle-square-square-square),
colors (red-red-blue-blue-blue), numbers (1-1-2-2-2),
and so on.

1

1 , 2 , 3 , ___ , ___ , ___ , ___ , ___ , ___

2

___ , ___ , ___ , ___ , ___ , ___ , ___ , ___ , ___

3

___ , ___ , ___ , ___ , ___ , ___

Mixed Review and Test Prep

4 Which car matches this one?

Ⓐ   Ⓑ   Ⓒ   Ⓓ

136 *Use after Investigation 2 (Twos, Fives, and Tens), Session 9.*

© Pearson Education, Inc. **1**

Make Rows of 10

Color one square for each dot in the grid below. Be sure to fill one row before starting the next row.

Family Connection

Today the class was introduced to **Roll Tens**, a game in which pairs of students collect interlocking cubes and group them in rows of 10 to fill a rectangular mat. Here, students color in the number of squares indicated by the dot cubes they "roll." If a row is not completely colored in after your child finishes coloring the correct number of squares, ask, "How many more squares will you need to color to complete this row of 10?"

1 You roll

How many squares should you color? ____5____

2 You roll

How many squares should you color? _____

3 You roll

How many squares should you color? _____

4 You roll

How many squares should you color? _____

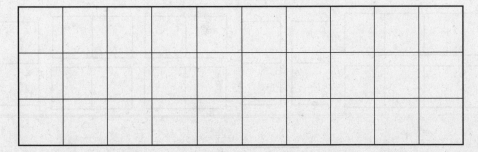

Name _____   Date _____

Number Games and Story Problems

Let's Count Squares

Write how many squares there are in all.

Family Connection

Students are learning to organize sets of objects (in this case, squares) so that they are easy to count and combine. In each of the exercises on this page, your child will need to decide what to count first: single squares, pairs, or strips. Talk with your child about the counting process he or she chooses to follow in each of the four exercises.

1

_____

2
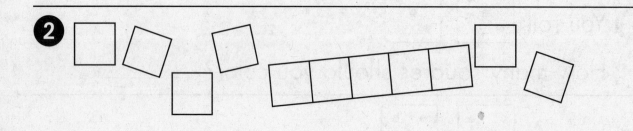

_____

3
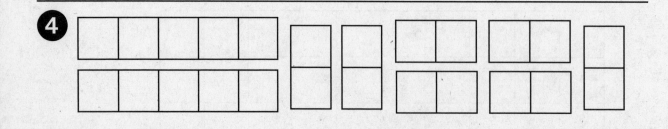

_____

4
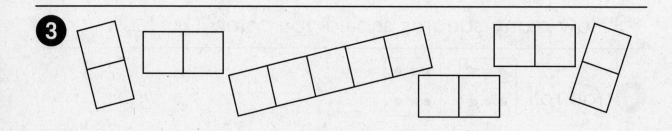

_____

© Pearson Education, Inc. **1**

138   *Use during Investigation 2 (Twos, Fives, and Tens), Sessions 10, 11, and 12.*

Name _____   Date _____

Another Look at Tens

Family Connection
Students continue to play **Roll Tens,** using cubes to fill a mat with 30, 50, or 100 interlocking cubes. This game helps students develop a sense of the relative sizes of numbers up to 100.

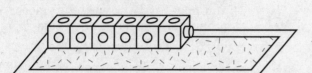

1 How many cubes are on the mat above? _____

2 How many more cubes do you need to make a row of 10? _____

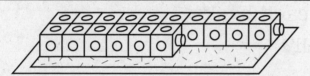

3 How many rows of 10 cubes each are on the mat? _____

4 How many extra cubes are on the mat? _____

5 How many cubes in all are on the mat? _____

Mixed Review and Test Prep

6 Which set of objects matches the number of dots on the cube?

Ⓐ   Ⓑ   Ⓒ   Ⓓ

Solve Some Problems

Use pictures, numbers, or
words to solve each problem.

> **Family Connection**
> Today students listened to a
> story that illustrated finding the
> total of several equal amounts.
> You might want to make up more
> problems like the ones on this
> page for your child to solve.

1 There are 3 leaves.

There are 3 ladybugs on each leaf.

How many ladybugs in all? _____

2 There are 3 baskets.

There are 5 apples in each basket.

How many apples in all? _____

3 There are 3 pots.

There are 10 flowers in each pot.

How many flowers in all? _____

4 There are 3 glasses.

There are 12 ice cubes in each glass.

How many ice cubes in all? _____

Mixed Review and Test Prep

5 How many students ride
the bus to school?

  5   12   17   22
 Ⓐ   Ⓑ   Ⓒ   Ⓓ

Do you ride the bus?

Yes	No
卌 卌	卌
卌 Ⅱ	

Use after Investigation 2 (Twos, Fives, and Tens), Session 13.

Combining Situations

Use pictures, numbers,
or words to solve
each problem.

Family Connection

Students begin Investigation 3 by learning more about combining situations. These types of problems involve a sequence of actions in which two quantities are combined. To solve story problems, it is important that your child recognize the sequence of actions in the story. This activity helps your child go through each problem step by step, focusing on what is happening first, next, and last.

There are 4 birds eating.
Two more birds come to eat.
How many birds are eating now?

1 How many birds were eating at first? _____

2 How many more birds came to eat? _____

3 How many birds are eating in all? _____

Three ducks are swimming in the pond.
Two more ducks join them.
How many ducks are swimming now?

4 How many ducks were swimming
in the pond at first? _____

5 How many more ducks came to swim? _____

6 How many ducks are swimming in all? _____

Separating Situations

Use pictures, numbers, or words to solve each problem.

Family Connection
Students are developing their understanding of separating problems—problems that involve one quantity being removed from another. Help your child visualize what is happening in each situation. Help him or her understand that when one amount is removed from another, the result is less than what was started with.

There are 4 butterflies on a leaf.

Three of the butterflies fly away.

Now how many butterflies are on the leaf?

1 Are there **more** or **fewer** butterflies on the leaf at the end of the story? _____

2 How many butterflies are on the leaf at the beginning of the story? _____

3 How many butterflies fly away? _____

4 How many butterflies are left on the leaf? _____

There are 9 ants on the sidewalk.

Five of the ants crawl into the grass.

Now how many ants are on the sidewalk?

5 How many ants are on the sidewalk to begin with? _____

6 How many ants crawl away? _____

7 How many ants are left on the sidewalk? _____

Number Games and Story Problems

What's the Sum?

Write the sum of
the two numbers.

Family Connection
Students are playing **Five-in-a-Row,** a game in
which they practice adding single-digit numbers
such as 5 and 3. If needed, provide something for
your child to use as "counters." Your child can show
each quantity and then combine the counters to
find the sum.

1 | 5 | 6 | _____

2 | 10 | 8 | _____

3 | 3 | 7 | _____

4 | 4 | 4 | _____

5 | 2 | 1 | _____

6 | 9 | 7 | _____

7 | 8 | 5 | _____

8 | 3 | 6 | _____

9 | 6 | 6 | _____

Mixed Review and Test Prep

10 Which block has the **most** sides?

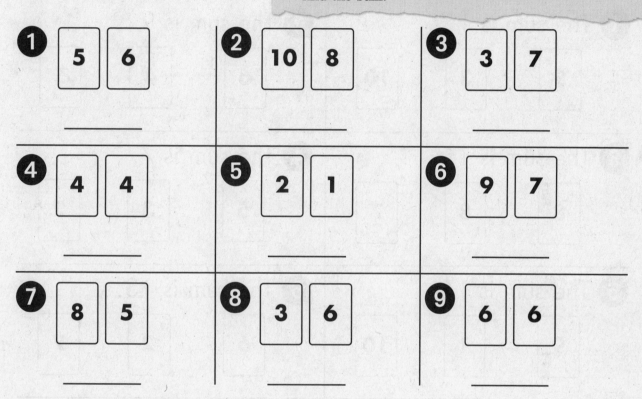

Ⓐ   Ⓑ   Ⓒ   Ⓓ

11 Which block has the **fewest** sides?

Ⓐ   Ⓑ   Ⓒ   Ⓓ

The Sum Is ...

Circle the cards that make each sum.

1 The sum is 15.

| 5 | 3 | 10 |

2 The sum is 9.

| 6 | 4 | 5 |

3 The sum is 16.

| 8 | 8 | 7 |

4 The sum is 7.

| 5 | 3 | 2 |

5 The sum is 11.

| 9 | 1 | 10 |

6 The sum is 13.

| 6 | 2 | 7 |

7 The sum is 4.

| 3 | 2 | 2 |

8 The sum is 20.

| 10 | 9 | 10 |

Mixed Review and Test Prep

9 How many cubes are in this pattern train?

| 11 | 10 | 9 | 8 |
| Ⓐ | Ⓑ | Ⓒ | Ⓓ |

Number Games and Story Problems

More Story Problems

Solve each problem. Show how you solved it.

1 Jon has 4 big boats and 7 little boats. How many boats does he have in all? _____

2 Jackie had 14 stuffed dogs. She gave 4 to Jenna. How many dogs does Jackie have now? _____

3 There are 5 red kites and 8 green kites flying high in the sky. How many kites are flying? _____

4 The clown was holding 15 balloons. 9 of them popped. How many balloons are left? _____

Can You Make 10?

1 Color each shape with a pair of cards that adds up to 10.

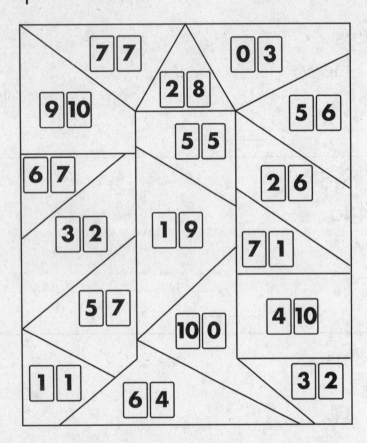

Mixed Review and Test Prep

2 What comes next?

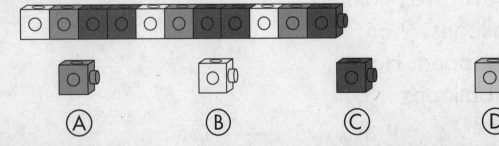

Ⓐ   Ⓑ   Ⓒ   Ⓓ

Number Games and Story Problems

What's Missing?

Each pair of cards should make 10. Write the missing number.

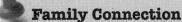

Family Connection

Students continue building their knowledge of number combinations by playing **Tens Go Fish** and **Five-in-a-Row.** Ask your child how he or she figures out what number card is needed to make 10. Does your child pick numbers at random and add them to find out if the sum is 10, or does your child "just know" some of the combinations?

1 | 8 | ☐

2 | 5 | ☐

3 | 1 | ☐

4 | 0 | ☐

5 | 6 | ☐

6 | 7 | ☐

Mixed Review and Test Prep

7 Which tower has the **most** cubes?

A   B   C   D

Ⓐ   Ⓑ   Ⓒ   Ⓓ

8 Which tower has the **fewest** cubes?

A   B   C   D

Ⓐ   Ⓑ   Ⓒ   Ⓓ

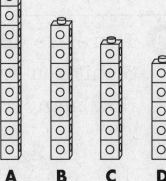

A   B   C   D

Number Games and Story Problems

Solve and Show

Use pictures, numbers,
or words to solve
each problem.

Family Connection
Today students solved combining and separating
story problems involving larger numbers (teens and
twenties) and shared their strategies for doing so.
Your child can solve the problems here in any way
that makes sense to him or her.

1 Angela had 21 stamps in her collection.
Then her grandpa gave her 4 more stamps.
How many stamps does Angela have now? _____

2 There are 10 goldfish, 3 black fish,
and 9 striped fish in the tank.
How many fish are in the tank? _____

3 There are 18 children in the class.
3 children are absent today.
How many children are present? _____

Number Games and Story Problems

How Many Marbles?

Use pictures, numbers, or words to solve each problem.

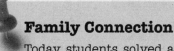

1 Marco had 4 marbles.

Then his brother gave him more.

Now Marco has 8 marbles.

How many marbles did his brother give him? _____

2 Ellie has 3 red marbles.

She has some blue ones too.

She has 5 marbles in all.

How many blue marbles does Ellie have? _____

3 There were 7 marbles in the jar.

Then Maggie put more into the jar.

Now there are 10 marbles in the jar.

How many marbles did Maggie put in the jar? _____

Number Games and Story Problems

Match to Make 10

Match cards to make a sum of 10.

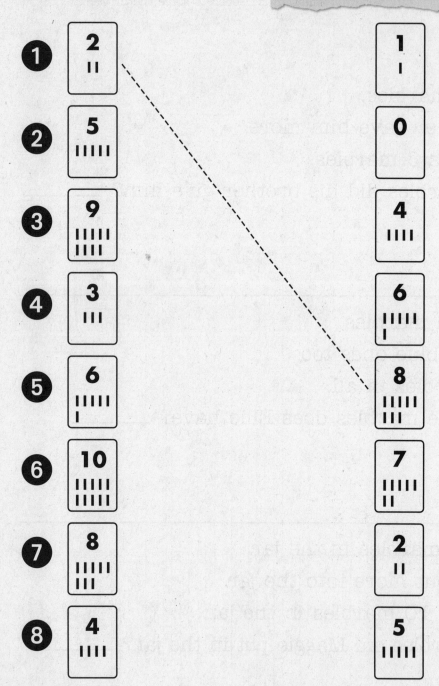

© Pearson Education, Inc. **1**

Name _____ Date _____

The Total Is 20

Circle the cards in each row that have a sum of 20.

Family Connection

Today students played **Total of 20,** a game in which partners, using 20 cards, take turns finding combinations of 20, such as 10 and 10; or 6, 5, and 9. Ask your child how he or she is determining which combination of cards in each row has a sum of 20.

1 | 10 | 5 | 3 | 10 | 1 |

2 | 5 | 8 | 2 | 7 | 5 |

3 | 2 | 1 | 6 | 4 | 9 |

4 | 3 | 5 | 2 | 7 | 5 |

5 | 2 | 7 | 9 | 8 | 1 |

Mixed Review and Test Prep

6 Which pair of cards has the largest total?

3 4	5 5	8 9	7 6
Ⓐ	Ⓑ	Ⓒ	Ⓓ

Name _____   Date _____

Make 20

Draw more number cards so that each row has a total of 20.

Family Connection

In class, students are continuing to find combinations of 10 and 20. In the activity on this page, students are given 2 or 3 cards, and then they have to show another card, or cards, so that the sum of all the cards is 20.

1 | 10 | 5 |

_____

2 | 2 | 7 | 3 |

_____

3 | 6 | 4 | 1 |

_____

4 | 8 | 9 |

_____

Mixed Review and Test Prep

5 Which animal does **not** belong in this group?

 Ⓐ   Ⓑ   Ⓒ   Ⓓ

Use after Investigation 3 (Addition and Subtraction), Sessions 10, 11, and 12.

Number Games and Story Problems

Solve and Show

Use pictures, numbers, or words to solve each problem.

Family Connection

Students are continuing to analyze and solve three types of story problems: ones in which amounts are combined and the outcome is the unknown (for example, 4 + 6 = ___); ones in which one quantity is removed from another and the outcome is the unknown (for example, 10 − 4 = ___); and ones in which two quantities are combined and one of the quantities is the unknown (for example, 4 + ___ = 10).

1 There were 12 apples in the basket.
Then Mick put 8 more in the basket.
How many apples are in the basket now? _____

2 There were 30 grapes in the bowl.
Chester ate 12 of them.
How many grapes are left? _____

3 There were 15 strawberries on the plate.
Then Mac put more on the plate.
Now there are 22 strawberries on the plate.
How many strawberries did Mac put on

the plate? _____

Bigger, Taller, Heavier, Smaller

Which Is Heavier?

1 Circle things that are **heavier** than a box of cereal.

toy boat   bike   spoon   penny

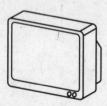  

television   chair   box of sugar   pencil

2 Find an object. Write its name. _____

Then write names of things that are **heavier** than the object.

_____

_____

_____

Name _____   Date _____

Look at Balances

Which side of the
balance is showing the
heavier object? Write **A** or **B**.

1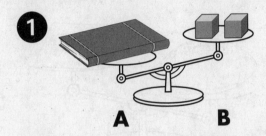

   A   **B**   _____

2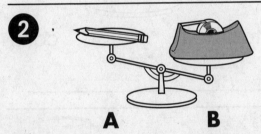

   A   **B**   _____

3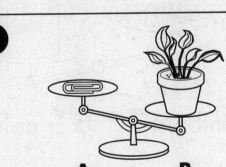

   A   **B**   _____

Mixed Review and Test Prep

4 Which block is used the most
in this design?

    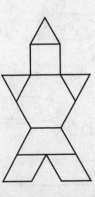

Ⓐ   Ⓑ   Ⓒ   Ⓓ

Bigger, Taller, Heavier, Smaller

This Is Heavier

Write the name of the object
that is heavier.

1

marker   book

_____

2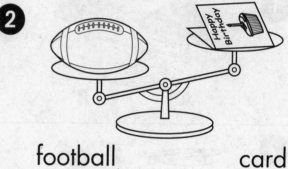

football   card

_____

3

bear   block

_____

4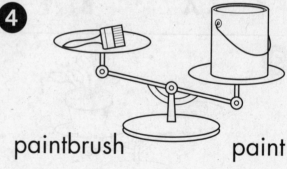

paintbrush   paint

_____

5

lunchbox   pennies

_____

6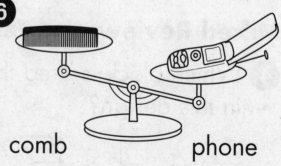

comb   phone

_____

Use during Investigation 1 (Weighing and Balancing), Sessions 3 and 4.

Bigger, Taller, Heavier, Smaller

Which Is Lighter?

Circle the name of the object that is lighter.

Family Connection

Students continue to use a balance to compare the weights of two objects. **Questions you might ask your child:** "Does a larger object always weigh more than a smaller object? In which exercise does the smaller object weigh more?"

1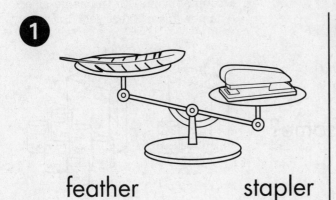

feather   stapler

2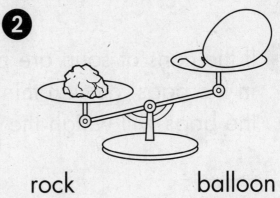

rock   balloon

3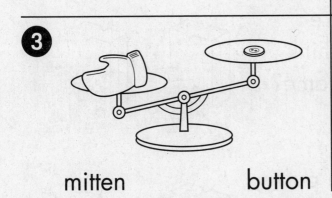

mitten   button

4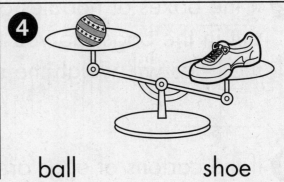

ball   shoe

Mixed Review and Test Prep

5 Each cube stands for one student. How many students are in school today?

19   20   22   23
(A)   (B)   (C)   (D)

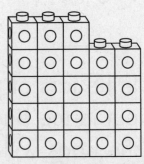

Students Here Today

Name _____ Date _____

What's in the Bag?

Write **yes** or **no** to answer
each question.

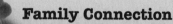

Family Connection

Students have been balancing
the contents of two grocery bags
so that each bag weighs about
the same. On this page, students
look at the contents of two bags
and decide whether they weigh
the same. If you have cans of
soup at home, all the same size,
demonstrate Exercise 1 for your
child.

1 If the cans of soup are put
in the bags, do you think
the bags will weigh the same?

_____

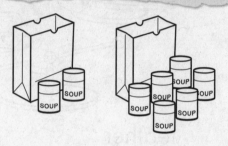

2 If the boxes of noodles are
put in the bags, do you think
the bags will weigh the same?

_____

3 If the cartons of eggs are put
in the bags, do you think the
bags will weigh the same?

_____

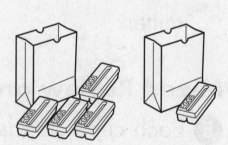

4 If the jars of peanut butter are
put in the bags, do you think
the bags will weigh the same?

_____

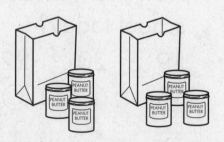

© Pearson Education, Inc. **1**

Name _____   Date _____

Make It Balance

Family Connection
Students have been balancing balance scales trying to make a balance **even.** On this page, students add cubes to one side to make the sides balance. Ask your child whether there is another way to make the sides balance.

1 Circle the balance scale that is even.

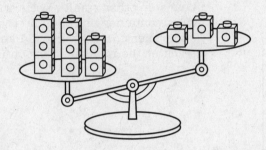 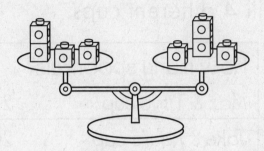

___

2 Look at the balance. Which group of cubes is heavier?

_____

3 To balance the two sides, which side would you add cubes to?

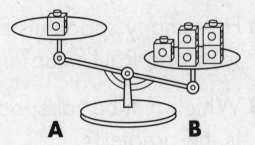

A   **B**

_____

___

4 Look at the balance. Which side has the lighter object?

_____

5 To balance the objects, which side would you add pencils or cubes to?

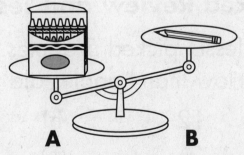

A   **B**

_____

How Much Does It Take?

The chart below shows how many spoonfuls of sand it took to fill 4 different cups.

Family Connection

Students have investigated how many spoonfuls of sand it takes to fill a small cup. You may wish to try something similar with your child at home. Have him or her estimate how many spoonfuls of beans or other small objects will fill a container and then do the experiment. Help your child keep track of the number of spoonfuls.

How many spoonfuls?	
Max & Tim's cup	27
Jake & Raul's cup	20
Ming & Tess's cup	15
Merrick & Maria's cup	24

1 How many spoonfuls filled Jake and Raul's cup? _____

2 Which number of spoonfuls is the greatest? _____

3 Which pair of students used the least number of spoonfuls? _____

Mixed Review and Test Prep

4 Jessie picked 5 apples. Claire picked 6 apples. How many apples did the girls pick in all?

12 11 10 6

Ⓐ Ⓑ Ⓒ Ⓓ

Name _____ Date _____

Bigger, Taller, Heavier, Smaller

Which Holds More?

Circle the container on the right that holds more than the first container.

Family Connection

Students have been comparing the capacities of two containers. Some students filled one container and then poured from that container into the other to see which held more. You may wish to show your child several containers at home and ask which holds more. Have your child make a prediction and then check it.

1 |

2 |

3 |

4 |

5 |

6 |

7 |

© Pearson Education, Inc. 1

Use during Investigation 2 (Filling), Sessions 2, 3, and 4.

161

Bigger, Taller, Heavier, Smaller

Fill the Shape

Write how many
of each shape fills
each outline.

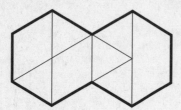

Puzzle 1

	Shape	How many?
1	△	
2	▱	
3	⏢	
4	◻	
5	◇	
6	⬡	

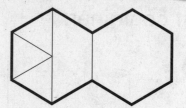

Puzzle 2

	Shape	How many?
7	△	
8	▱	
9	⏢	
10	◻	
11	◇	
12	⬡	

Bigger, Taller, Heavier, Smaller

Which Holds the Most?

Put each group of containers in
order. Write **1** for the smallest one,
2 for the middle-sized one, and
3 for the biggest one.

Family Connection
To develop the idea of
capacity, students have
been filling two different
containers with sand and
deciding which container
holds more. Show your
child two containers and
ask him or her which
holds more.

1

_____ _____ _____

2

_____ _____ _____

3

_____ _____ _____

4

_____ _____ _____

5

_____ _____ _____

Bigger, Taller, Heavier, Smaller

How Much Does It Hold?

1 Draw a line to match the containers that hold about the same amount.

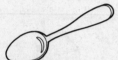

2 Name two other things that you think hold about the same amount.

_____

Mixed Review and Test Prep

3 Which cube train is the shortest?

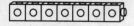   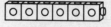

    Ⓐ   Ⓑ   Ⓒ   Ⓓ

Name _____ Date _____

Solve the Riddles

Write the letter of the container that solves the riddle.

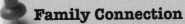

Family Connection

Students have been comparing how many interlocking cubes different containers hold. You may wish to find several small containers at home and have your child show you how he or she can determine which container holds more by filling the containers with beans, paper clips, other small objects, or sand.

1 I have more than 20 cubes.
I have fewer than 40 cubes.
Which container am I?

A.

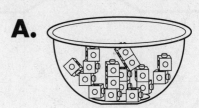

_____

2 I have between 1 and 20 cubes.
I have more than 10 cubes.
Which container am I?

B.

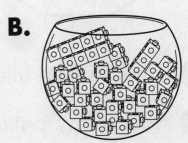

_____

3 I have more than Container A.
I have more than Container C.
Which container am I?

C.

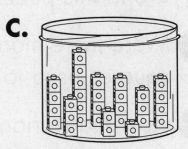

_____

4 I have fewer than 25 cubes.
I have between 1 and 10 cubes.
Which container am I?

D.

_____

Name _____   Date _____

Take a Close Look

Use this completed Block Puzzle
to answer the questions:

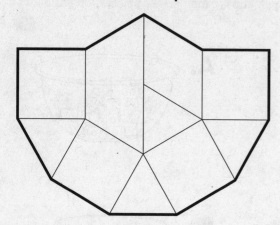

Interesting Tidbit

Did you know that the Epcot
Center in Florida is shaped
like a ball but is made up of
triangles? Such a building is
called a **geodesic dome.**

1 Is the outline filled? _____

2 How many pattern blocks
are in this puzzle? _____

3 Were there more trapezoids or more
squares used to fill the puzzle? _____

4 How many triangles were used? _____

Mixed Review and Test Prep

5 Hannah ate 4 crackers. Harumi ate 5 crackers.
How many crackers did the girls eat in all?

11   9   7   1

Ⓐ   Ⓑ   Ⓒ   Ⓓ

Name _____   Date _____

It's Longer

Circle the longer object.

1

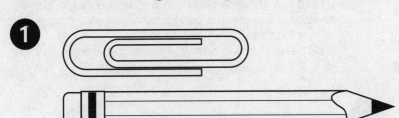

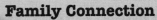

Family Connection
Students have been comparing the lengths of pairs of classroom objects and have identified the longer object. You may wish to have your child compare a spoon with different objects and determine which object is longer. Make sure he or she is aligning the two objects on one end before comparing their lengths.

2

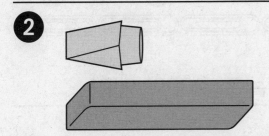

3

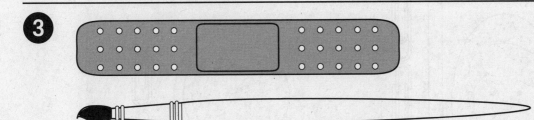

4

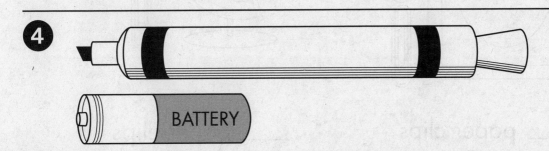

5

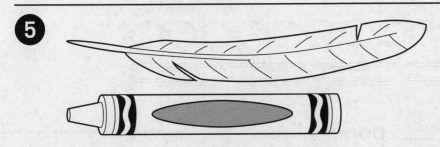

Bigger, Taller, Heavier, Smaller

How Long Is It?

Write how many paper clips long or high each picture is.

1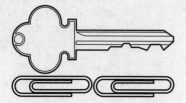

_____ paper clips

2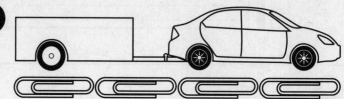

_____ paper clips

3

_____ paper clips

4

_____ paper clips

5

_____ paper clips

Bigger, Taller, Heavier, Smaller

Put Them in Order

Put the items in order. Write **1** for the shortest. Write **2** for the middle-sized one. Write **3** for the longest.

Family Connection
Students traced and cut out feet of different lengths and then ordered them from shortest to longest. Your child might enjoy repeating that activity with people in his or her family.

1

_____   _____   _____

2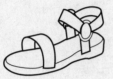

_____   _____   _____

3

_____   _____   _____

Mixed Review and Test Prep

4 Which group shows more stars than the group at the right?

Bigger, Taller, Heavier, Smaller

Measure with Squares

Write the number that
tells how many squares long
or high the picture is.

Family Connection
Students measured the lengths
of objects with interlocking cubes
and then ordered the objects by
their lengths from shortest to
longest, or from longest to shortest.
Ask your child to name the objects
on this page in order from shortest
to longest.

_____

_____

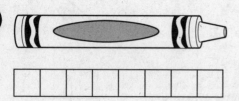

_____

 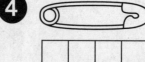

_____

 Name an object that is shorter
than the crayon in Exercise 3.

_____

Mixed Review and Test Prep

 Which shape does not belong in the group?

   Ⓐ   Ⓑ   Ⓒ   Ⓓ

Name _____   Date _____

Shortest to Longest

Look at Bars A, B, C, and D.

Family Connection

Students have been using pictures, numbers, words, or any combination of these to represent objects and order them from shortest to longest, or from longest to shortest. Ask your child to explain how he or she accomplished this task in class.

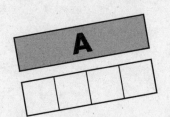

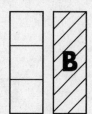

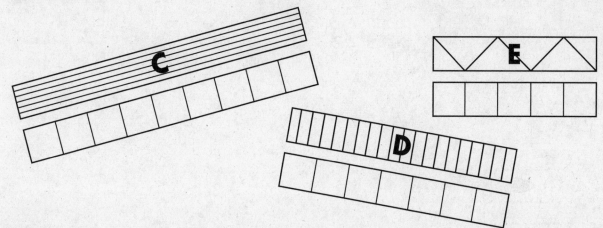

1 How many squares long is Bar C? _____

2 Which is longer, Bar A or Bar E? _____

3 Write the letters of the bars in order from shortest to longest.

_____ _____ _____ _____ _____

Mixed Review and Test Prep

4 How many more counters are needed so that there are 10 counters in all?

    4   6   8   10

    Ⓐ   Ⓑ   Ⓒ   Ⓓ